Bye-Bye, Fatty Patty

Bye-Bye, Fatty Patty

Patty Hullett

To order additional copies of this book, contact:
Xlibris
1-888-795-4274
www.Xlibris.com
Orders@Xlibris.com
777547

Contents

CHAPTER 1

"Fatty Patty Becomes Part of Me"

Patty is my name. The following is my story, and I'm sticking to it.

I am first and foremost a Christian, so I've never paid much attention to horoscopes or prophetic things, except where the Bible is concerned. However, I do find it quite ironic that my zodiac sign is Libra, "the sign of the scales". You see…..I'm a very unique person that has lost over 500 pounds. Oh, no -- not all at the same time, but over the years that I've spent as a fat person on this earth, I've lost a ton of weight. Fighting the "Battle of the Bulge" has been a life-long engagement for me. I've definitely "been there and done that" – many, many times.

I have been overweight since birth, being yanked into existence by my mother's favorite OB-GYN doctor who I'm told proudly announced that "we've got a big girl here". His initial judgment turned out to be correct, as I weighed-in at just under ten pounds, and this became my first bad, recorded experience with the dreaded "scales". So, being fat is certainly not new to me. Over the years, being overweight became my mantra, my truism, the person who I really am. And for approximately 55 years of my life I've tried practically every fad diet and weight lost method known to man. That means that I've pretty well run the gambit of programs and products like…..various types of over-the-counter pill appetite suppressants, Adys (a candy appetite suppressant from the sixties), doctor-prescribed diet pills (heavy amphetamines), Weight Watchers (too many times to count), clinical hypnosis (which was a joke to me), citrus diet, Sego and Metrical nutrient shakes (that were pre-cursors to today's Slim-Fast products), grapefruit diet (that left me with hives for a week or so), and even underwent TWO major weight-loss surgeries -- just to name a few of my numerous failed attempts at successfully losing weight and keeping it off.

I don't really remember too far back in my early childhood years and I don't think I even realized that I was an overweight child until I started the first grade in 1961. I had never even heard the terrible rhyming play on my name, "Fatty Patty". But it wasn't too many weeks into my early school days until I became acquainted with this type of bullying or name-calling that hurt me very deeply. Thinking back now, I can still faintly hear some of the kids standing around at recess and calling my name out......

"Fatty Patty, two by four,
Can't get through the bathroom door,
So, she did it on the floor,
And it stunk forever more."

To me, this little rhyme wasn't playful and fun at all. This one was very personal and it wounded me every time I heard it. It was in the first grade that I heard that nickname for the first time, and it has followed me around most of my life like a ghost --- "Fatty Patty". So, it was a fact that I weighed 94 pounds in the first grade and now you understand how I became "labeled".

This may sound quite harmless to some people, especially in today's world where bullying seems to be totally out of control. But even back in the sixties, this type of ridiculing made me feel like there was something genuinely wrong with me. And as a result, it made me consider myself as different than the other kids. I think I was around six or seven years old when "Fatty Patty" came to reside inside of me. She kind of became my alter-ego, or somewhat my inner self that helped me deal with stressful situations brought on by my feeling of being inferior or not as accepted because of my size.

Back in my childhood years I was somewhat of an oddity. Most first graders weighed between 40 to 60 pounds. In that day most mothers didn't work outside of their homes either, and more home-cooked meals were the norm. The three main meals – breakfast, lunch and dinner – were made by the mom in most cases. Not many alternative choices were available to us back then. Instead, today we opt to choose convenience over smart meal selections. We often tend to choose the easy-the-way-out eating path, where we pack-on the unwanted pounds by fast-fooding our way into an unhealthy living style. The results are often obese children (and adults), because of the high-calorie fast foods that we choose to rely on and that are so easily accessible today.

Living my life as an overweight child, I sometimes pondered why my mother would have named me something that would cause me such grief. Why in the world would she have dubbed me "Patty"? I was not Patricia, but instead, plain, old "Patty". Didn't she realize that "Patty" would rhyme with "Fatty", and there became the focal point of my demise (or so I thought in my mind). Actually, she explained to me that she never dreamed that I would be overweight, so it was just an odd coincidence.

I can remember the kids sometimes calling me *"Fatty Patty"* and my inner self would raise her ugly head inside of me, sometimes to give me courage, but more often than not, to join in to make me feel even worse. ***"Don't raise your hand to answer your teacher's question! The kids will all look at you and make fun, especially if you give the wrong answer! Surely you don't want to risk that kind of embarrassment."*** So frequently I would change my mind and not participate in the classroom discussions. I, many times, chose to remain silent when I really wanted to be a part of things.

Because I felt so fat and because of some issues I was dealing with at home, I sometimes began to hear the voices more and more, from inside my head. Things like......

"I didn't get chosen again to be in the class play because I am too fat."

"No one ever picks me to be on their team because they think I'm too lazy and slow."

These *"Fatty Patty"* flashbacks didn't happen too often in my grade school years. I pretty much tried to be everybody's friend and that kind of kept me insulated from some of the kidding. I was so super-sensitive that I tried my best to get along with everybody. Sometimes that made me disguise my true feelings, as I became somewhat of a people-pleaser.

"The disease to please," as psychologist Harriet Braiker likes to call it, is a form of addiction. Just as a <u>drug addict</u> seeks drugs, a people pleaser seeks approval. As I got older, I became more of this type of person.

According to Dr. James C. Dobson's 1999 reprint of his book *"The New Hide or Seek"*.........

> *"We are not what <u>we</u> think we are.*
> *We are not even what <u>we</u> <u>think</u> others think we are.*
> *We are what <u>we</u> <u>think</u> others think we are."*

Dr. Dobson claims, "There is great truth in this statement".

Also, being overweight added extra pressure in the smallest of daily things, to the point of being somewhat of a perfectionist. I had a mother that tended to hold her approval just out of my reach, no matter what I tried or how successful I was at attaining my goals. I could never seem to completely satisfy her. She always wanted just a little bit more out of me. I think by the time I was in the third grade I already had myself so wound-up about making straight A's, that I was sometimes a nervous wreck about tests, report cards, class rankings, etc.

Not only did my mother put pressure on me, but I put pressure on myself. I felt that I had to somehow find a way to make-up for being overweight. So, I thought I should be twice as good as the other kid, just to be able to be accepted.

Every year in my elementary school, the nurse would weigh each student and record his/her weight on the report cards. This was the most treacherous day of the school year for me. There was no being discreet in the sixties. The nurse weighed me in front of everybody, and then would vocally call-out my weight to her assistant that would record the numbers. I was totally mortified when they would announce to the world how much I weighed. I remember my weight, year-by-year, and the numbers were never good.

1st – 94 lbs. (and keep in mind that most first graders weighed somewhere between 40 - 60 lbs.)

2nd – 112 lbs.

3rd – 121 lbs.

4th – 135 lbs.

I sometimes reminisce about the days when my favorite and very obese uncle would come to our house for a visit. He loved to talk and laugh out loud, the kind of contagious laughter that made everybody join in, even if they didn't know what had made him laugh in the first place. He would bounce me on his lap and ask me, "What are you going to do if you get too fat and can't find a boyfriend?" He loved it when I would quickly reply, "I'll just find me a FAT boyfriend!" Problem solved.

Every August, in our small town, we anticipated the annual Lions Club carnival. It was an event that most of the population turned-out for, and it was always just before the start of a new school year. The three-night festival highlighted games like Bingo, cake walks, ring toss, pick-a-fish, water-dunking booths, etc. The kids loved all the carnival rides, but the adults seemed to favor the bands performing nightly on the big stage. The adults would bring their own lawn chairs from home and find a choice spot so they could enjoy the musical entertainment.

I recall one summer evening in the early sixties when my father encouraged me to join some of the kids participating on the stage in the new fad dance contest, where the band was featuring the music of the "Twist". It was the latest dance craze and my daddy, the dancer that he was, had already taught me his best rendition of Chubby Checker's new dance moves.

As it turned out, they asked me and three other children (all probably under the age of ten) to come on up on the stage and we had a "danceoff". It never occurred to me at the time, that everybody was laughing and clapping for me --- not because I was a great dancer like my daddy had convinced me, but rather, that the audience was enjoying the little fat girl making a fool of herself on the stage that night.

A couple of years down the road, when I was a little older, I would attend the annual carnival, but since that time, I had grown very aware of my size and how easy it was for people to make fun of me for being overweight. No one found me entering anymore public dance competitions, once I woke-up and realized that people can often be cruel.

Unfortunately, I think I just happened to have the "fat" genes from most of my mother's side of the family. A lot of them were either overweight, or big-framed, or both. When we'd have a family reunion and all get together to visit, I was always amazed how BIG some of my kin folks were.

Many of us, me included, resembled an "Overeaters Anonymous" group gone completely wrong.

My mother, bless her heart, tried her best to watch over me and to monitor my eating when she was at home with me. She always worked an office job every day, so she was only "on duty" as my diet monitor every week day evening and on weekends. I've never been a good liar and this helped make me a pretty honest kid. It seemed like every time I would try to tell a little white lie, my mother always seemed to find out the truth anyway. Since I was never much of a sneaky kind of kid, it surprised me that I would sometimes find myself tiptoeing back into the kitchen after dinner time to get a quick snack (of course, without my mother's permission).

There was one little deceitful time that I remember very distinctly. My grandmother kept my sister and me every school day while my mother worked. She usually prepared the weekday evening meals for my entire family. One evening we had enjoyed some home-made meatloaf that was particularly good. My sister and I generally played outside until dark, so I think back to one night where I scoped-out the kitchen area. No people were to be found anywhere. My grandmother had already gone home and my parents must have been out in the den watching TV. There was only the stove light on in the kitchen, so the lighting was very dim. I spied some of the remaining meatloaf on a paper plate on the stovetop. I quickly snuck into the kitchen, grabbed a big handful of the meat with my bare hand, and then scurried back outside. I made it out the back-screen door, and then plopped the hunk of meat into my mouth. Boy, did I get the biggest surprise of my life! It turned out to be our dog's food on the plate and not the delicious meatloaf. I started spitting and gagging, trying to throw-up the awful-tasting dog food (which was probably horse meat). Yuck, and double yuck! What a hard way to learn a hard lesson about being deceitful. Believe me, I didn't try to pull another one of the sneaking food stunts again (unless there was adequate lighting for my food thievery).

And then several things happened to me in the 4th grade that forced my mother's hand to finally try to do something very drastic to help me.

CHAPTER 2

Who Likes Santa Claus Anyway?

In the fall of 1964 I decided to give the Girl Scout organization a try. That seemed harmless and perhaps the new activity might offer some much-needed self-esteem. I was so excited to be a part of things and looked forward to ordering my uniform, just like all the other girls. A major obstacle became a new problem, as my mother and I came to the stark realization that I couldn't fit into any of the sizes available in the regular children's catalog. It became appallingly apparent that I would have to be fitted for a Den Mother's (ladies') outfit. That could certainly ruin your day, knowing that you could only be outfitted in the adult ladies' clothing.

From there we encountered more complications, as we had to find a seamstress that could cut-off about 14 to 16 inches of the material on the bottom of the Scout Master's dress, and then the shoulders hung off my frame to make matters even worse. To complete this somber fashion look, I realized that I had to wear one of those awful-looking berets on my head. I wasn't certain, but I could almost bet that one of those kinds of hats would prove to be very unbecoming on the head of a very chubby-cheeked fourth grader that weighed-in at 135 pounds.

I guess I was so excited to be a part of things that I totally skipped the fact that I looked horrible in this Girl Scout get-up. I wasn't aware of how bad I looked until we got our individual class pictures back. The day that the photographer had arrived, was also my scout meeting day, so I had to wear my uniform. When my school teacher handed-out the picture packets a couple of weeks later, I was so ashamed of what I saw when I looked at the fat girl in the picture, that I was crushed.

I always genuinely loved everything about school during my first three years of elementary – except for Physical Education class. The P.E. teacher didn't seem to like overweight children, or so it appeared to me. From time to time we had to participate in an inside tumbling class held in the gymnasium. The children lined up and she forced us to try different types of tumbling exercises on long, cushioned mats placed on the gym floor. She was kind of mean most days, and so the kids started calling her "Miss Crab-Apple", instead of her real last name – "Crabtree". I completely detested the idea of me attempting all sort of ridiculous things that I had no way in the world to be successfully do because of my size. I could somewhat manage a front somersault, but the back one was a near impossibility for me and my chubby body. Cartwheels were most every little girl's delight, but I wasn't a fan of this tumbling exercise at all. Not wanting to embarrass myself, I often tried to be absent on days that we were scheduled to do the tumbling or calisthenics (body exercises performed without apparatus). I just was not good at the strenuous exercises that took a lot of bending or squatting. Believe me when I tell you, that I was not being lazy. I was simply too fat to accomplish the feats Miss Crab-Apple wanted me to be able to do.

Surprisingly, I generally did well at the outdoor activities. I thoroughly enjoyed the P.E. baseball games, kickball, tetherball, etc. As far as the playground exercise went, I could easily swing, play on the Jungle Jim, and see-saw, but sometimes Miss Crab-Apple would make us try to go across the monkey bars for a grade. I would get up there and hang on the first bar, and I would literally have tears streaming down my face, with her prodding me to swing my little rotund body in the effort to move one of my hands onto the next bar. I was never, never, ever able to do the monkey bars. All I thought this playground apparatus did was humiliate me in front of my schoolyard buddies.

By the time the class Christmas party was rolling around in 1964, I became even more devastated. My fourth-grade instructor, an extremely favorite teacher of mine, disgraced me so badly that I went home crying one day. This was just a few days before Christmas. Mrs. Alfred called me up in front of the class and asked if I wanted to play Santa Claus at our party the next day. I took this to mean that I was the obvious choice since I was the fattest kid in my class. I remember running home, crying all the way.

When my mother got home from work she could tell from my red, swollen eyes that something had upset me. She asked me what was wrong, and I unloaded the whole story on her, which sent her blood pressure up and this immediately prompted her into the other room to call this uncaring and insensitive teacher right away. After about thirty minutes of waiting for my mom in the den, she came in and tried to explain the situation to me. She told me that Mrs. Alfred was so terribly embarrassed that she had offended me, that I had made the highest grade on a test that day, so she thought that would be an appropriate award – for her to offer me the honor of playing Santa Claus and handing-out the presents at our party the next day. Needless to say, I still was not on-board with this suggestion at all, so I drug myself to school the following morning. My mother let this teacher know, in no uncertain terms, that I would not be playing the role of Santa after all. "Merry Christmas to all, and to all a good night!"

That was such a black cloud time of my life that my mother decided to do something drastic to help me lose weight. In the mid-sixties she had heard that many people in town were losing large amounts of weight, in an unbelievably short amount of time. Enter in – the "quack" diet doctor......

Mother made an appointment with this infamous doctor in Dallas, and before you could say "diet pills", I was taking very strong, addictive amphetamines, thyroid pills, as well as fluid injections and fluid meds. I would say that is some pretty hefty stuff for an eleven-year-old girl. These diet pills often kept me awake at night, and I was so wired during the day that I could hardly sit still. I became a nervous wreck, chattered all the time like a magpie, sometimes suffered from hallucinations, often experienced heart palpitations, had frequent headaches from eating too little, and my hands shook so badly that I could hardly write at school. But.......the one, good thing that came out of this exercise in futility, was the fact that **I DID LOSE WEIGHT! I dropped about 35 pounds in a five or six-month span. The bad thing was that once I quit taking the pills, I quickly put most of the weight back on. But that led me to a positive "next" step in my weight-loss journey.**

I flashback to days of almost driving my mother totally batty...... I would announce about every ten minutes that I was bored and she needed to give me something to do. However, I did realize that my school work had improved. I had to keep constantly "busy" or I drove myself and everybody else crazy.

Some days I would feel a little faint, and that always concerned me. Also, when I would take part in handwriting exercises in class, I noticed that my hands would sometimes shake like an old person's.

In case you can't tell from my description, I was taking speed from this "quack" of a doctor. Years later, I would come to realize that the pharmaceutical amphetamine that I was taking was actually "black mollies", or so they were called on the street. These were extremely dangerous, heavy amphetamines that were a potent central nervous system stimulant. Very often "shady" doctors prescribed these diet pills for people desperate to lose weight quickly. However, this course of weight-loss action usually just masked the real problem of most of their patients. Their attempt to lose weight was unsuccessful because of their diet choices and lack of exercise. Also, it became a known medical fact (after a while) that continued use of these diet amphetamines could cause serious health problems long term.

I was no dummy, even when I was taking these pills at the age of eleven. I realized that there was no way that I could continue taking these risky "uppers". There just had to be a better way to lose weight. However, I do recall one day toward the end of school in the fourth grade in 1965. This was truly a milestone in my life, even if it were a one-day, short-lived moment of success. Unbelievably, I weighed-in at 100 pounds. It was just one day, but what a day that was – especially realizing that I hadn't achieve a weight that low since I was in the first grade (1961-1962).

CHAPTER 3

Whirling, Twirling Dervish

Later in my grade school years, I tried something else that would prove to be life-changing for me and my suffering self-esteem. I had a cousin named Judy that had become a part of a local dance and twirling studio in town. She was a couple of years older than me, but she seemed to really like taking baton twirling lessons. My mother devised yet another plan for a possible way to lose some weight. She decided that she would let me <u>try</u> the baton lessons, if I would <u>try</u> to lose some weight. Thus, I became one of the "Lancaster Starlettes", under the direction of Miss Chris Ellis, an accomplished dance and twirling instructor. Long story short, it became one of the best moves of my life.

Not only was I losing a little weight, but I was gaining much more confidence in myself and in my twirling abilities. I started out in group lessons, but after a while we began competing in outside competitions in our twirling and dance teams. We were rolling along very well and doing quite admirably in twirling contests across the State of Texas.

I would often go to these outside contests, in cities like Dallas and other surrounding areas, and just sit there for hours watching the other girls that competed in individual events, not the "team" events that my group was a part of. I became so obsessed with watching these girls that performed "solo" twirling routines, that I begged Miss Chris to teach me a routine so I could compete individually. After several months of learning and practicing my own two-minute routine, I got up the nerve to compete at a Dallas area event – all alone.

I was so, so nervous before I went in front of the judges, that I had to run back to the restroom to throw-up first. I splashed some water in my face, then returned to the gymnasium and waited for my name to be called. I marched up to the judge's table and twirled my little heart out for almost two minutes. I felt like I had done a pretty good job on my routine, and I had completed all my tricks without dropping my baton one single time. After all the girls in my age division had finished their routines, the judges deliberated and made their final selections for the top five places. I'm thinking that there were about 10 or 15 girls in my age group. At the end of the day of competition, the judges called all the participants back and asked the girls to take a seat on the gymnasium floor. They began to call out the groups awards first, and then next, the individual awards. When they came to my division, I couldn't believe that they actually announced my name as the 1st place winner in my 11-12 age group.

That's all it took. By winning a 1st place trophy home at age twelve, I was totally hooked on baton twirling – and it was hooked on me. The next few years found me placing high even in State competitions, and eventually it even qualified me twice to compete at national meets. This meant that I got to travel all over the country during my twirling years, thus making me feel that I was becoming "OK" as a person. I had developed a real skill that made me feel better about myself.

The only minor set-backs were at times when I remember things like...... (1) marching in a parade and I'd hear someone in the crowd say, "Look at the fat girl at the end of the line"; OR (2) during one contest when a competitor's mother approached the judges' table and started ranting and raving about how they could have picked "the large girl in the pink uniform" – instead of her little darling. My mother heard just enough of the story to get herself involved in the confrontation. She got her two cents worth in when she retorted, "The judges' decision is final, so you need to butt-out. Besides, my *large* girl in the pink, just flat-out beat your little *skinny* girl in the blue." My mother seemed to be my eternal defender and protector where my weight problem was concerned.

Ironically, the contest director threatened to call the Dallas Police Department if the two mothers didn't settle down. This could have proven to be quite embarrassing for everyone, especially since this twirling contest was being held in downtown Dallas at the humungous First Baptist Church gymnasium.

Thankfully, my baton teacher Miss Chris turned-out to be another life-long encourager that helped build me into a confident young girl, and then, later on, turned me into a polished and fearless teenage performer. She and her husband never had children of their own, so her baton girls were almost like her own kids. Often, she would let a large group of us girls spend the night at her mansion-like house. It was always fun and exciting at Miss Chris' house. She had a colorful parrot that would keep us awake all night by talking in short, funny phrases that made us laugh. Also, she had an over-zealous, protective Chihuahua dog that did not take to overnight guests. We would have to move around the house carefully because any sudden motion would make the dog nip at our heels. We literally had to quietly tip-toe around or the tiny attack dog would be all over us.

The best thing about Miss Chris was that she was the coolest chaperone ever. Since she really didn't know much about raising kids of her own, she would often let us do kind of dangerous stuff. It was never anything that really put us at risk, but she often pushed the edge of the envelope where childrearing was concerned.

I remember one time, in particular, when we were away at baton camp for a week at The Dells, Wisconsin. Because we had such a large number of girls from our same twirling studio, we were able to stay together in our very own large, private cabin. One night, Miss Chris ordered pizza to be delivered to our secluded cabin for a special evening treat. Once the two cute guys came to our front door, she insisted that they come inside and have some pizza with us silly, giggling girls. It was just the neatest thing ever. None of our parents would have ever let that happen. It was a blast, all because of Miss Chris and her lenient rules. We loved her!

During the week of the same camp, she kept reminding us that we were spending too much money on souvenirs, T-shirts, etc. We still had an overnight lay-over in Chicago on our way back to Texas, so she urged us to be careful to save enough money for us to get home safely. Just as she had cautioned us, at the end of the week we arrived in Chicago with us girls living on very limited funds. When we realized how expensive our hotel restaurant charged for meals, we then knew what Miss Chris was trying to warn us about.

She said that all of us girls had created the food and money problems ourselves, and that we would now have to just pick the cheapest thing on the menu for the remainder of the time that we had to stay in the high-priced hotel in Chicago. Most of us didn't have extra money, so we were basically "stuck like Chuck". I'm sure that Chris had plenty of money that she could have loaned us, but instead she was teaching us a valuable lesson about being careful with our spending money.

The very cheapest thing on the menu turned-out to be strawberry shortcake, which was priced at about $2.50. That was nothing for us to really worry about......... We all liked strawberry shortcake and we could eat it a few times for breakfast, lunch, and dinner. At breakfast, it was delicious. At lunch, it was ok, but not very filling. At dinner we were starving, and Miss Chris had ordered herself a wonderful-looking fried chicken dinner that she was going to eat right in front of us. Wow! The smell was driving us so crazy that none of us could focus very well on our third-time serving of strawberry shortcake.

About the time we were finishing up our dessert/meal and feeling sorry for ourselves, in came more waiters because of Miss Chris ordering all us girls the same fantastic fried chicken meal, along with all the trimmings. We were so excited and appreciative of her generosity, while at the same time we were learning a hard lesson about traveling and living on a budget.

So, you can understand how we thought Miss Chris was the most fun adult that we had ever been around. However, on a more serious personal note, she not only taught me how to twirl a baton very well, but she also poured many life lessons into me that would serve me well, later on in life.

When I turned 17, she even guided me into setting up a baton twirling business for myself in another city. There was no way that I ever wanted to "compete" with her, but she gave me all the tools and motivation that I would need to get my own business off the ground. I successfully ran my own twirling studio for over eight years and made a lot of good extra spending money from my craft. Over the years, I've probably trained several hundred girls from the ages 4 to 18 on how to twirl those amazing batons.

Miss Chris and I were close friends over the years, even up until her death in 2005. I was so honored to be able to speak at her funeral service in our hometown of Lancaster, Texas. She was a one-of-a-kind special lady, and one of the most influential people that I've ever met. She literally gave me "courage" to be able to successfully handle myself at ANY weight, big or small. And I'll ways be a proud member of the "Lancaster Starlettes" twirling team, who were the National Champion Dance Twirl Champions in 1966. We won that honor during our trip to the University of Ole Miss, in Oxford, Mississippi. And several girls that I twirled with for many years are still some of my best friends in life. We had formed life-long relationships, bound by our love and comradery for baton twirling based on our growing-up time with Miss Chris.

Some years later, after I had closed my own studio, I decided that I might want to go back to teaching baton twirling for a large dance studio. At our first meeting, I handed the business owners my twirling resume which included my national team recognition, my individual solo accomplishments of being qualified to participate at Nationals in St. Paul, Minnesota two years in a row, as well as my adult kudos as a selected twirling judge at the national "America's Youth on Parade" competition in South Bend, Indiana during the late 70s. I also wanted the dance owners to know that in 1968, I had the honor of winning the one-baton and two-baton championships for the A.A.U. organization.

However, I could somewhat read the faces of the man and woman owners and could feel their hesitancy over hiring an overweight baton instructor. I then spoke-up and told them that I would be happy to briefly perform an exhibition of my twirling skills. They instantly nodded their approval and I showcased my one-baton solo routine where I did a series of tricks, finger-twirls, horizonals, rolls around various parts of my body like the waist, legs, elbows and shoulders, and even bounced the baton off my neck and one of my legs, etc. I then I bent over to pick up my second baton, and proceeded to introduce them to my ability to keep both batons moving while completing an array of fancy tricks. Lastly, I concluded my act by impressing them with my juggling skills.

Both owners, as well as some of the children and parents had now joined us in the large classroom and they now clapped with such enthusiasm that

I knew I had proven myself worthy for the job of baton twirling teacher. There again, I was having to prove myself because of my size.

After spending a couple of years with the dance people, I realized that I was having to work way too hard (10 classes a week) to have to split my earnings with the dance studio. I completed my classes there and then set-out to find a more profitable way to pick-up some extra money with my baton lessons, while maintaining my regular secretarial job during the day.

Next, I met with several of the recreation departments of small surrounding towns in the area where I lived. Now my twirling class would be a part of each city's recreational program. That way, I had a great facility to teach in at one of their nice, local gymnasiums, and I got to keep all my hard-earned money for myself. It was a kind of win-win situation for me.

However, I faced the same sort of scrutiny again when I started signing-up the children for my new classes that were being formed. One of the fathers even had the audacity to ask me "who" would be teaching the baton lessons. I defiantly told him, "I am the baton teacher, and if you want to stick around for a few minutes I will be doing a twirling exhibition for any of you that might be doubters".

Just like before, as with the dance owners, I showed my twirling skills and immediately felt their genuine approval. In fact, the same father came up to me later and said, "Yes. I can certainly see that you ARE the baton teacher." He congratulated me on my performance, and I enjoyed a couple of very successful years of teaching in four different city recreational programs.

I don't have an exact number of students that I taught over the years, but I would guess at least five hundred. That meant that every time I went to the grocery store, or attended a local sporting event, or shopped in any of the surrounding towns, I inevitably I would hear some little girl's voice yell out, "Hi, Miss Patty", and that always warmed my heart.

CHAPTER 4

"And the Beat Goes On"...
Featuring Fashion Malfunctions
and Minor Meltdowns

With my mother working at the main mail order offices of Sears, Roebuck and Company in Dallas, Texas, and during my school days, she tried her best to try to keep me in the groove by dressing me in the latest fashions. It wasn't always so easy for non-standard sized girls back in the sixties and seventies, but my mother gave it all she had. There was also a large retail Sears store within the same facility where she worked, so my sister and I were always blessed with the most up-to-date clothes, toys, and other memorabilia as we grew up. We were always the new kids on the block that had the most unique toys like: a truckload of the latest dolls, a full-sized Chinese rickshaw, a miniature player piano, and white mink stoles, complete with little red high heel shoes --- just to name a few. Watch out, Marilyn Monroe......

I recall when Beatle Mania had taken the world by storm. I was but a mere 4th grader, but I had Beatle fever in a bad way. I was especially smitten by the gorgeous Paul McCartney. I even got in a physical, rolling-on-the-playground fight with my best girlfriend Becky because she argued that John Lennon was cuter than Paul. Come on...... Give me a break. Paul was definitely the heartthrob of the group.

The "Fab Four" from Great Britain had also influenced fashion in a big way, and even boys' hairstyles at the time. Almost every guy wanted long hair like The Beatles, and the girls wanted wigs to join-in the fun.

There was just something magical about this group. I think back to making shopping excursions to Dallas with my mother. There was one big store, Sanger-Harris department store, that was stocked with Beatle merchandise. I would save-up my hard-earned allowance and beg mother to make a trip to Dallas so I could shop for anything "Beatle" --- wigs, posters, T-shirts, pennants, buttons, etc. The kids, especially teenagers, had gone stark, raving mad over the four talented guys and their different music.

I literally begged my mother to take me to see them in concert when they came to Dallas September 18, 1964, but she was not having any of it. She kept telling me that I was just too young for a concert like that. Just so you know...... I still have not forgiven my mother for not taking me to that Beatle concert in 1964. They only made one trip to my city, and I missed my one chance to see them. I was broken-hearted.

The fashions from Carnaby Street, a shopping area in Soho, in the City of Westminster, Central London was the latest craze. I remember how groovy I must have thought I looked when my mother came home with a Carnaby-style outfit – complete with empire-waist black plaid dress with matching knee-high socks (to be worn with penny loafers) and an English-looking hat, called the Liverpool / Breton, mod style cap, often worn by Beatle John Lennon. It was a wonder that the kids in my class didn't laugh out loud at me, right to my face, but I thought I had it going on!

I remember one day in the fifth grade that my mother brought me home the latest fad -- a "paper dress". I couldn't wait to wear it the next day at school. Note to self: A paper dress was not meant for a tomboy girl. During P.E. that day, I tore my beautiful, floral dress under my arm, and it continued to rip downward. I knew that leaving the school playground area was against the rules, but I lived just across the street from the baseball field, where we often hung-out during recess time. I simply snuck across the street, ran into the house, had my grandmother help me find another dress to put on, and back onto the school property I went! Luckily, nobody told on me.

In the sixth grade I started on my mother about taking me to see the new TV band that was now touring, The Monkees. I had to be there at this concert. After all, I was the President of my town's Monkee Fan Club. We held our meetings at the local Dairy Queen. Isn't that where all the important meetings took place in my little quaint town?

I finally convinced mother to take me to the hottest show in the town, so my first official, first-ever concert was to see The Monkees, not the Beatles. My mother had a better time than I did at the show. She was having a ball laughing at all the sites surrounding her. There were girls screaming and crying, some were kissing the photos from their souvenir booklets that were being sold, and various other weird things were being thrown onto the stage by the out-of-control audience – things like phone numbers, plush animals, flowers, etc.

So, while all this craziness was going on around me, I was happy and becoming an adolescent. I was shocked, but I kept my weight down to an almost normal size during the fifth and sixth grades. The 35-pound weight loss from the diet pills kept me motivated to stay active, and I continued with my baton twirling that helped a lot, too.

It was the very first few days of my entering junior high school that I totally embarrassed myself. I was a new seventh grader at a very old, antiquated school. In fact, my mother had gone to this very same school back in the late forties, when the buildings actually held students from the first through the twelfth grades. That should help you understand why the students not only used these same old dilapidated facilities, but they had also placed several army type barracks on-site to accommodate the over-crowding of the regular school buildings.

It seemed like every year in junior and senior high school, there was always at least ONE cute male teacher that sent every girls' heart into an irregular beat. Call it love or call it premature lust, but it was definitely something.

This ONE teacher was especially flirtatious with the junior high girls. In fact, he liked to hand out licks for simple things like forgetting your colored map pencils, or coming in class ten seconds after the last bell rang, or any other incidental little thing that he could come up with. He would literally bend the girls over (with dresses on) and then rub the paddle across their behinds several times before he would deliver a quick and meaningful swat with his famous paddle.

In today's society, that would be considered sexual harassment and could have resulted in lawsuits or even the said teacher might have been fired from his position. But it wasn't even reported back in my time in the late sixties.

It happened to be raining that ominous day in early September. I, as well as half of the seventh-grade girls, had a huge crush on our new Texas History teacher. He was young and good-looking, and it was rumored that he was single, as well. I remember the day, almost like it was yesterday. Some things just stick in your memory. I had on a new brown polka-dot "tent dress", with brown suede baby-doll shoes. I thought I was looking especially stylish that day, or I was, up until the moment I went running from one of the regular buildings, up some stairs, and into the doorway of Mr. Skinner's history class that was held in one of the army barrack buildings.

I crossed the threshold in my brand new, flat-bottomed shoes, and I guess the rain had made the floor especially slick as well. I slid about five yards into the classroom. Once I realized that this was not a bad dream, that this was happening to me, I looked around and heard the laughter of the other kids. Not only was that humiliating to me, but as I got up and dusted myself off, I looked and Mr. Skinner was laughing the loudest of all. Once he could get this breath back from all the laughing, he told me to go onto the restroom and gather myself.

I slowly walked from the classroom and somehow found my way into the girls' restroom. I looked at myself in the mirror and burst out crying. Not only did I have a skinned-up knee which was now bleeding, but I had also messed up my new beautiful dress. I stood in the bathroom for almost the full hour of history class, not wanting to go back, and I certainly did not want to face Mr. Skinner. Thirteen-year old girls that had crushes on their teacher were not supposed to go sliding into the class for obvious reasons!

CHAPTER 5

Time for a Change

It was the summer before I entered the 9th grade, and I had become increasingly aware that I had put some extra pounds back on. My fondest desire was to be able to try-out for the majorette line in my high school, but I knew that would mean more dieting by me and my poor mother. Always on the lookout for new things to try, my mother had come upon a relatively new weight-loss program for us to attempt, Weight Watchers ("WW"). She took me to a local church where the weekly meetings were held. We were entertained and inspired by a WW lecturer who was a success story herself. She explained how the diet program worked, what foods and what amounts we could eat, and then finished her session by sharing some of her own "fat" stories that so hit-home that I couldn't believe others were suffering from being "fat" just like me.

I was so taken-in by the lecturer's motivating speech that I lost a whopping 7 pounds the very first week. Getting some weight off right off the bat drove me even more to follow the food plan as closely as I could. After a while though, my biggest nemesis for derailing my weight-loss program turned-out to be my sweet and loving grandmother. My dear Granny Smith was so nurturing and caring that she would worry about me not getting enough to eat. I would have the correct portion size of the vegetables and meat that I was supposed to eat at a meal, but she would come back and offer more.

Granny would say things like, "I know that's not enough food to keep anybody alive. I'm scared you're going to get sick if you don't eat more." I was often strong enough to tell her "no", but sometimes I would still be a little hungry, so I would oblige her request and eat something extra. I justified this in my mind, that by eating a bit more I had just made her feel better. Also, I thought this would give me a green light to cheat, at least a tiny bit.

My kind little Granny was an old-school, Southern country cook that didn't know how to serve a meal without potatoes. Her Idaho culinary repertoire included mashed, boiled, baked, French-fried, scalloped, and good old fashioned "fried and steamed" potatoes. She would call my mother at work some days and complain that she couldn't find anything in the house to make for dinner. That didn't really mean that we were out of food choices. It just meant that we were out of her favorite staple – potatoes. If that wasn't fattening enough, she often chose to "fry" all the meats and then she would complete the meal with a good, fatty gravy or sauce to add-on even more calories. Believe me, Granny was an excellent cook, but preparing healthy meals was just not her thing.

Regardless of Granny's interference, I was extremely successful at losing some weight. And I did enjoy going to the weekly WW meetings, but I always felt odd because I was about the only kid there. I saw lots of overweight men and woman, but it was strange to see any children (even teenagers like me) at the weekly weigh-ins and meetings. Also, I sometimes suffered from the same kind of indignation, just like when I used to hear my weight called-out during my grade school years. School nurses were not the only ones that didn't seem to realize that calling out your weight was terribly painful and hard to bear. Thankfully, over the years, the WW people wised-up and started covering up the top of the scales and became more discreet in recording everyone's numbers. In later years, this made the weigh-in process much more private. But in my early years of WW experiences, the old "call out the weight for everybody to see and hear" method was used, despite my crushed feelings.

I do remember a few little food stories that my first WW lecturer told us. She comically reminded us that an overweight person usually starts eating a pie in this way....... First a sliver, then a slice, then a slab. And before you know it, the entire pie is gone.

The same type of thinking is used when watching a fat person eat French fries. A normal person would generally eat one fry at a time, and he/she would actually chew up the potato strip in their mouth. This is not the usual case for a fatso, and I'm including myself in this group. I realized that when I ate fries, like from McDonald's, I grabbed two or three fries and ate them all at one time. (I guess my thought pattern was that I should eat them as quickly as possible so they wouldn't get cold, or maybe I ate several at a time so my friends or family would not ask me to share my fries.) I always seemed to find justification in how and when and in what quantity I ate my food.

The lecturer also asked her class members if they often ate their cake batter before they poured it into the cake pans. I smiled when she told us this one, as my mother would sometimes ask me why I prepared only one-layer cakes. I can't imagine where the extra batter would have gone. Sometimes I would eat so much of the cake mix and icing while making the cake, that I wouldn't really want to eat a piece afterwards. I was already full of the taste before it was even done.

I must definitely give serious "kudos" to WW because it really is a good, solid, healthy weight-loss plan, and it did work for me every time I tried it and stuck to it. My problem would be hitting a plateau along the way, where I would basically follow their instructions and would only lose a pound or less. That was always so discouraging and would make me give up after a while if I only experienced very little weight loss. My beat-down mentality was always...... "Why keep eating and following their strict rules if I'm not really losing much weight?" Often times, I would quit going to the meetings, and before I knew it, I had quit eating the correct foods. I quickly went back to my old, bad eating habits.

After a couple of months, I'd go back to the meetings and join again --- only to lose 20 or 30 pounds and then hit the dreaded "plateau" again. After struggling through the eighth grade, I was able to get down to about 130 pounds, and that meant that I was weighed-in and became "acceptable" to participate in the majorette try-outs prior to entering the 9th grade in high school. The selection process for twirlers was under the direction of the high school band director. And that spelled "bad news" for me.

At the majorette try-out day, I felt I did myself proud. I was the only one, out of about 10 or 12 girls that completed their routine without dropping the baton one, single time. The judges gave me the highest marks of the competition, but because I was only a freshman, they gave the Head Majorette position to one of my older friends (Denise) that was a junior classification at our high school. I had no problem with this. I was just so happy to be able to be a part of the majorette line. All of the chosen girls had already been my friends at Miss Chris' local baton studio, so I felt like I fit right in. And I was so ecstatic to be a Lancaster High School twirler, that my self-esteem really took-off during my teenage years.

The one rain cloud that seemed to hang over me (and a few of the other majorettes) was the fact that the band director didn't want any overweight twirlers marching in front of his award-winning band. Three or four of us girls tended to be ten to twenty pounds overweight, and he had been very clear that he was "not going to have a fat majorette marching in front of his band". And I could tell that he meant every word of his statement.

I absolutely loved being a part of my school. I was busy, busy, all the time. From early morning and after school band practices, to twirling lessons at Miss Chris' studio, to attending school club meetings, participating in weekend parties, etc. I felt that I was somewhat a "normal" person with a vibrant, exciting life, and I loved "almost" every minute of it.

What I didn't like about high school was that the band director always seemed to be like a food Nazi watching over me. I remember him coming through the school cafeteria some days, and he'd front me out by asking what I was having for lunch that day. Most of the time, he would have nothing to say back after I told him that I was following my WW food plan. And while most of the teenagers sitting around me were enjoying their fattening hamburgers, French fries, pizza, etc., I was choking-down my delicious (?) dry tuna sandwich (with the vegetable oil soaked through the bread), a pickle, and an apple or orange for dessert.

I had to basically follow the WW plan at least about 75% of the time, or I would start gaining weight back. The band man made me feel so worried all the time. I often feared that he might make me weigh at any given time, just to be able to kick me off his majorette line. I never felt like he really liked me anyway, and I always thought it might have been because I was not that great of a musician. My saxophone capabilities were not the greatest, so I think he leaned on me harder than maybe some of the other majorettes that also had minor weight problems.

CHAPTER 6

Life with My Alcoholic Father

The seventies were quite a ground-breaking decade that provoked more openness in sensitive matters on television shows. Two of the most famous and eye-opening programs were *"All in the Family"* and *"Maude"*, both produced and largely the brain children of the controversial producer Norman Lear.

Quoting from Wikipedia, "The American sitcom TV-series, *'All in the Family'* was originally broadcast on the CBS network for nine seasons, from January 1971 to April 1979. It starred Carroll O'Connor, Jean Stapleton, Sally Struthers, and Rob Reiner. The show revolved around the life of a working-class bigot (Archie Bunker) and his family."

Wikipedia continued, "The show broke ground in its depiction of issues previously considered unsuitable for a U.S. network television comedy, such as racism, infidelity, homosexuality, women's liberation, rape, religion, miscarriages, abortion, breast cancer, the Vietnam War, menopause, and impotence. Through depicting these controversial issues, the series became arguably one of television's most influential comedic programs, as it injected the sitcom format with more dramatic moments and realistic, topical conflicts."

"Maude" is an American sitcom that was originally broadcast on the CBS network from September 12, 1972, until April 23, 1978.

Also, according to Wikipedia, "the *"Maude"* TV program starred Bea Arthur as Maude Findlay, an outspoken, middle-aged, politically liberal woman living in suburban Tuckahoe, Westchester County, New York, with her fourth husband, household appliance store owner Walter Findlay (Bill Macy). Maude embraced the tenets of women's liberation, always voted for Democratic Party candidates, and advocated for civil rights and equality. However, her overbearing and sometimes domineering personality often got her into trouble when speaking about these issues."

So, if you can get an inkling of the personae of these two TV characters, then you might better understand my household situation. If you can, please imagine Archie Bunker and Maude, the two of them, together as husband and wife --- and there you have a visual of my parents butting heads all the time. That is what turmoil I lived in many days of my life.

Most weekdays my construction-worker daddy would come home late from work, after stopping by a bar to drink a few beers. My parents would then yell and scream a lot, sometimes he'd make my mother cry, and occasionally she would even try to call the police on him, but they would struggle and he would ultimately get the phone away from her. While all of this was going on, my sister and I would stand by crying, just wanting them to quit yelling at each other. Both parents would threaten to leave each other, but I was the forever peacemaker that would always beg them to stay together. I didn't want to have to choose between my mother and daddy. I wanted us to be a family – a regular, normal, let's all get along kind of family.

My daddy never hit my mother, nor did he ever physically harm us in any way --- but when he was drunk his verbal abuse was out of control. Experts say that the mental scars are much more lasting then those that are physical.

I became a fingernail biter at an early age and I still bite my nails today, as a chronic, nervous habit.

Interestingly enough, in 2017, I completed some in-depth, self-research and found out why I might be the way I am today.

Per Dr. Janet Woititz, the author of her 1983 bestselling book, *"Adult Children of Alcoholics"*, she says, "Children who grew up in an alcoholic home develop similar personality traits and characteristics." She further claims, "Alcoholism is a family disease; and we often become para-alcoholics and take on the characteristics of that disease even though we did not actually pick up the drink".

From her book…..

Here are some of the <u>Characteristics and Personalities of Adults Who Grew Up with Alcoholism in the Home</u>

1. <u>Fear of losing control</u>. – They want to maintain control over their behavior and feelings. They also try to control the behavior and feelings of others. They do this out of fear.
2. <u>Avoid conflict</u> - They are constantly seeking approval of others.
3. <u>A high burden of responsibility</u> - They are oversensitive to the needs of others. Their self-esteem comes from others' judgments of them, often they are perfectionists.
4. <u>Adopting compulsive behavior</u> - They may eat compulsively or become workaholics.
5. <u>Abandonment issues</u> - They will do anything to save a relationship, rather than face the pain of abandonment even if the relationship is unhealthy.

All these characteristics still very closely describe me. There's no wonder I'm such a mess sometimes.

My dad had been involved in a construction job accident during my 9th grade school year. It was a terrible thing, as he got one of his hands caught in a machine. His co-workers had to rush him to a nearby hospital, with another man carrying his glove which contained his five fingers that had been cut off. Amazingly, the doctors were able to save all the fingers, except for the thumb. After a while it just wouldn't seem to heal, so they finally had to amputate about two-thirds of his thumb. Every one of the other fingers involved in the accident was almost as good as new.

My dad had started to take me around town to look at possible used cars for me to drive back and forth to school. I felt so lucky because I think I was about the oldest teenager in my sophomore class, since I had a September birthday. That meant that I got to drive first, and I might have also even been the first in my class to get a car of my own! Call it a "God" kind of coincidence, but I had my eyes set on a good-looking 1966 blue Chevy Malibu. It belonged to an older teenage boy, so the back of the car was jacked-up some; it had wide racing tires on it, and very cool mag wheels. To make it even more appealing, it was my favorite shade of royal blue. And it really sounded "mean". The asking price of this used car (back in '69 or '70) was the unbelievable amount of $900. Well, we kept waiting for my dad's insurance company to send him his accident settlement check. The day the check arrived I almost died. The check was for $900, the exact amount that I needed for my used car!

A couple of years later when my younger sister was needing a car of her own, my dad mused, "What am I going to have to get cut off this time so we can afford a car for your sister?"

It was not easy growing-up as a teenager in my alcoholic domain, but for the most part, life was at least bearable. I had such a fantastic time my freshman year of high school, that I couldn't imagine even more fun as I turned sixteen. Life was good, especially as driving and dating were added into the mix of my new responsibilities and privileges.

In 1969 and early 1970 I had gone out on a few dates, but mostly they were "double" dates or we connected in group settings. I had dated around a little, had been kissed a few times, had been forced to use my hand-to-hand combat training on a couple of hormonal guys, but nothing serious at all, no real sparks. I just enjoyed getting to be out and to be a part of the dating scene.

Then something happened to me in the fall of 1970 that changed my life forever. I loved being a part of the high school football games on Friday nights. The majorettes marched in front of the band at halftime, and then we were usually featured in a spotlight twirling routine while the band played the music for us.

It was during one of those football games that I spotted a nice-looking boy on the sidelines. I think that we kind of made eye contact, so I mentioned him to one of my friends that the guy was really cute. Well, it didn't take long for that little tidbit to get around to him, and about a week later I got a phone call from him.

It didn't take long until I was in full-force, head-over-heels love with my new heartthrob. He was not just any heartthrob. He eventually became THE ONE for me!

Unfortunately, my daddy would sometimes catch me coming in from a date, and of course, he was full of liquor. He would try to pick a fight with me for no apparent reason. He would say unsavory things and make unfounded accusations about our relationship and what we did out on our dates. His favorite thing was to ask me why I would want to go out with a "hippie".

I would then ask him, "What is a hippie, Dad? Is he considered a hippie because he has hair hanging down over his shirt collar? Does that immediately make him a bad person because he has long hair?"

Then, we'd go on and on arguing until I could finally get him to shut up where I could go on to bed. I learned, after time, that it was better for everyone in the house that I should try to sneak in, get undressed as quickly as possible, and then get in my bed and act like I was asleep – so he couldn't accomplish starting another fight about my boyfriend.

You see, my dad was a labor union construction worker, a steamfitter to be exact. A steamfitter is a person who installs pneumatic tubing, just like the tubing at the drive-up banks. You know, where you press the "send" button, and the vacuum power sucks your deposit into the waiting bank receiving port. That was his occupation, one that paid very well, considering that he was forced to quit school in the eighth grade because of family financial hardships. He was the youngest of eight other brothers in his struggling, dirt-poor family.

Over the years, my dad became a kind of a stereo-type construction man. That is not to say that all construction workers are "A" typical like my dad, but a lot of them, are. But when my dad completed his eight hours and at the end of his work day, he and a lot of his buddies often stopped at a near-by beer joint/tavern/club (whatever you want to call it) and downed a few cold ones. Those were the days that his beer-drinking became a daily part of his life (and my family's life as well). Coupled with the daily drinking, he was a heavy cigarette-smoker, too. One fall afternoon I think a combination of the drinking, smoking, and bad eating habits landed him in the emergency room of one of the largest hospitals in Dallas.

He made it through the ensuing open-heart surgery, but never seemed to bounce back and feel like his old self ever again. He tried to go back to his old occupation in construction work, but he just couldn't focus, and his hands had become shaky and unreliable. Sadly, that left him nothing to do but retire in his early forties!

This life-changing revelation to quit his job put him even more into the throws of alcoholism. He lost much of his own self-esteem. The new situation compounded an already horrible situation, as he had no real hobbies, no non-working friends to pal around with, nowhere to go, nothing to fill his time doing, and no venues to spend his alone time during the days. It basically left him nothing to do but drink.

This love for beer quickly turned into the need for harder liquor. Before we knew it, he woke up and started drinking --- something of a "good morning" Bloody Mary to get him going. He would read the daily Dallas newspaper from front to back cover, but once he finished that task, his days (and nights) were spent in consuming alcoholic beverages.

Unfortunately, my alcoholic father never got better. Over time, he got much worse. His drinking only intensified, and it wasn't long until the beer-drinking turned-into consuming large amounts of hard liquor like vodka and gin. I could see him going down all the time. The doctor had very strict rules that he was to immediately quick smoking cigarettes and give up the booze. Neither of those medical demands were ever accomplished by my addicted father.

My mother and father started having more and more fights all the time. It became a very unpleasant place to be. Thank goodness, I was in high school and kept myself continually busy with anything to keep me out of the house and away from all the fussing and fighting between my parents.

It was about this time that my dad was around the house every day and he started giving me grief about my up and down weight gain. He declared that it should be a simple thing to lose the weight I needed to --- once and for all. (And, of course, his suggestions always happened while he was in the midst of one of his drunken stupors.) He suggested, in no uncertain terms, that I should "just push myself away from the table". That was his easy solution in a nutshell, according to James (my father). Totally offended by his one-sided, uncompassionate request, I challenged his authority by responding....... "I'll make a bet with you. I'll stop over-eating, if you stop drinking, and we'll just see who wins!"

My dad had nothing to say in retaliation. I had struck a nerve. He knew he couldn't quit drinking, I knew he couldn't quit drinking. In fact, anybody that really knew him, knew that he couldn't quit drinking. So, score one small point for Patty. The difference in my dilemma and his was that he didn't have to drink to live, but I did have to eat. The real problem stemmed from WHAT and HOW MUCH I chose to eat. And that was not such an easy thing for me to deal with. In fact, it was a daily struggle --- my plight to make good, healthy food choices.

I recall one hot, summer night, when a bunch of the teenagers in our neighborhood were sitting out on the sidewalk in front of our house. It was almost midnight (the curfew time for all of us). We were just sitting there, with our legs crossed "Indian-style" and gabbing. We were talking about everything or just nothing at all. We were just filling our time until our parents called us in for the evening.

I knew it was about time for my dad to return home from the local VFW Post, his almost nightly local beer-drinking place to get drunker. About that time, we looked down the street a couple of blocks away. My heart broke, and everybody saw what I saw --- my dad's white pickup truck being towed away by a police wrecker. No one said a word. Completely humiliated, I went running into the house to wake up my sober and sleeping parent, my faithful and responsible mother. She had to be told that my father was being transported to the local jail. There was no doubt that the offense would be "Driving While Intoxicated" (DWI).

Don't get me wrong, I loved my daddy with all my heart, especially in his early years of parenting, before beer (B.B.). He was a happy-go-lucky kind of man, always whistling a tune, or ruining the lyrics of a perfectly good song -- on purpose. All my friends became part of his nickname game. Becky was "Becky-Wecky", Vicki was "Vicki Sicky", etc. He even lovingly called me "Big Heavy". Those were definitely good times for me to focus on and remember. He even coached my girls' softball team a couple of years, and I think he's the one that cultivated my over-the-top love for sports. Even in my early grade school years, I was an avid high school and Dallas Cowboy football fan. I did love my daddy......... I just didn't like what he had become and what his drinking had done to our family.

I didn't know then, but I do know now that my mother should have divorced my father years ago. She took so much verbal abuse from him, that it was unbelievable. But, I also knew that she wanted to be able to keep our family living the same sort of lifestyle that we were accustomed to. Even at the age of sixteen, I knew that we would not be able to make it financially without my dad's income, so she somehow toughed it out. My mother always thought of my sister and me first. I think that was the biggest reason why I loved my mom so much. Over the years she took so much of his embarrassing behavior and alcoholic backlash, and she endured it all for the sake of her children.

Sometimes my daddy would mortify us in other ways in public. He would come to the high school football games loaded. He'd get extremely loud-mouthed and make a fool of himself, or sometimes he might even stumble or fall getting up or down the bleachers. It would be during these embarrassing times that I learned to be a very convincing actress.

My sister used to call me "Patty Perfect" --- and that was what I was always pretending to be. I had to be a "perfect" student (nothing less that straight A's). I had to give-off the air that I came from a "perfect" family. I wanted people to think that I had the "perfect life", etc. Nothing could have been further from the truth, but I pulled it off as best I could.

CHAPTER 7

Almost Love at First Sight

October 3, 1970 – My date had the cutest puppy-dog eyes I had ever seen, as I peered out the thin curtains covering our front porch windows. He was totally handsome, but I could tell that he looked like he was scared to death. My mother made it to the front door first, and there was my somewhat "blind date" Don standing there at attention. I rushed into the living room in the attempt to save him. I quickly introduced him to my mom. She gushed like a new Texas oil well. And then, off we went into the fall evening, as she gave us the standard dating instructions, curfew time of midnight to be strictly adhered to, and advice to drive carefully and have a good time.

He seemed to be shy and inexperienced, which I was personally happy about, since my last couple of dates fell into the "fast" type of guys. This boy looked timid, so I felt confident that I should be able to handle any situation that might arise that night. This date was going to be a piece of cake……..or so I thought.

Well, that was my initial intuition as we got into his car. He drove a very cute Ford Mustang, with the gear shift in between the two front bucket seats. "Oh, no", I thought to myself. This jerk already had a pillow sitting between the seats, indicating that he wanted me to sit next to him (already)."

Hadn't we just officially met for the first time, like five minutes ago? A red warning flag went up immediately in my subconscious.

Note to self: I really had this Don fellow pegged to be the sweet and innocent type, but perhaps I was wrong. Anyway, the first words out of his mouth, as we pulled out of my driveway, quite frankly concerned me, too. Quickly flashing me a sideways glance, he stated very matter-of-factly, "We're meeting some of my friends, another couple, in two hours. But until then, we'll just have to get lost and find something else to fill our time."

That statement didn't hit me very well. I really did not know this guy at all, only that he was in the grade ahead of me in school, and I had no idea of what kind of reputation he had. What my inner Fatty Patty voice said inside my head was, "Get ready, Patty....... I'm afraid he may be taking you to a motel for a quickie!"

Boy, did I get the wrong vibes from this guy. I braced myself for what next, I might encounter. I knew I must remain in control of my dating situation, even if I had to punch the guy in his gut, and take-off running.

Somehow, as we headed into downtown Dallas, Don began to loosen-up a bit, and we began to talk sports. Jock-types usually liked me, 'because I could talk football, baseball, basketball, just about any sport with the expertise and ease of a television sportscaster. I often knew the local scores, whatever the sport, and I could discuss the current roster names and moves, upcoming opponents, etc. So, we seemed to hit it off on that front. Check the first red box --- I passed the "she knows sports" category.

I also loved his selection of music on his car radio. We even kind of sang along to a couple of songs that we both liked. Check box number two --- he passed the "same taste in music" category.

Next, we talked about our high school and found out that we had some mutual friends, so that turned out to be a positive thing. Before I knew it, we were driving down some of the downtown well-known avenues. From there, we ended up in the northern part of the city where Southern Methodist University ("SMU") sits. He pointed out some of the landmarks there and almost two hours had flown-by without us even knowing it.

However, we traveled only a few more miles on the other side of the freeway from SMU, and I experienced a welcomed relief when he guided his Mustang into the parking lot of a very nice, upscale Mexican restaurant called "Trini's". The place was named after Trini Lopez, a Dallas-born singer, guitarist and actor that was popular in the 60s and 70s. Thankfully, Don just happened to be kidding about us getting lost for two hours. Nothing shady about him after all. Things were going along exceptionally well for a first date, and a kind of blind date at that.

Minutes later we were joined by one of his football buddies and his girlfriend. I didn't really know either of them well, just kind of who they were. We exchanged some high school chit-chat and enjoyed a very delicious dinner together. From there, we all drove to a downtown Dallas theatre called "The Majestic". We saw a hot movie for that time during 1970, "Angel Unchained" with Broadway Joe Namath and Ann Margaret. It was ok, not Academy Award-winning at all, just a good movie for a first date and with new friends. The movie concluded, we all said our good-byes, and both guys headed their cars back to our little town about fifteen miles south of Dallas.

Don seemed to want to kiss me goodnight when he pulled his Mustang into my driveway, but I guess he thought better of it. He slowly walked me to the front door. He was so nervous that I couldn't really tell if he was going to kiss me or not. After all the worrying about him being a "fast" kind of guy, and now I turned-out to be the one that was disappointed because he hadn't even tried to kiss me goodnight.

It got very still and quiet on the front porch. Thank goodness, my mother hadn't left on the porch light to illuminate this very awkward moment. Don told me how much he enjoyed going out with me, and there it was --- our first sloppy, half-missed my mouth kiss. He quickly turned on his heels and told me that he would call me the next day, if that was ok.

Just as I was about to step inside of the door, I hear laughter coming from the nearby bushes. Great! Two of my neighborhood girlfriends had seen the entire weird goodnight kiss in all its glory. At once, both girls start asking me if I liked Don. I told them that I couldn't really say yet. I did offer-up that I couldn't see me going with a guy named "Don" (kind of a lame name), and I also confided that he had a strange kind of voice. That was two strikes against him, right off the bat. However, I did like his taste in sports, in music, and in dining. Also, he was willing to spend some money on me, so that should count for something! Oh, well. I concluded that I would try to sort things out better tomorrow.

And besides, that really hacked me off that my friends were eavesdropping on my first goodnight kiss from Don. Could it be that they were jealous? As far as I could tell, they didn't seem to have any dates on that particular Saturday night!

Well, I didn't have to wait until morning, because Don had already made it home and picked-up the phone and called me around 12:30 a.m. So, I guess technically it <u>was</u> the next day. He seemed to be more confident over the phone than in person. We talked about this and that, and everything in between. I didn't get off the phone until about 4:00 that morning. I think we must have made a definite love connection.

For the first time in my life I felt like I was falling in love. In reality, at the ripe old age of sixteen, I truly had met the love of my life, my soul mate --- Don Hullett. And to think that it all started with a sloppy, sideways kiss – while my nosy friends looked-on from the front porch bushes.

CHAPTER 8

"Time to Toe the Line"

It was so strange that after we had been going steady for a couple of months, it occurred to us that we were doing the exact same thing. He thought he was too fat for me, and I thought I was too fat for him. So, what were we doing? Both of us started losing weight, as we were kind of starving ourselves and skipping meals, while never admitting to each other that we were both in the midst of enduring self-imposed diets. And we all should have known that starving ourselves was an impossible way to live.

After we got to know each other better, we could express our true feelings, and it became a joke that both of us were trying to become "skinny", each one for the other one. I guess the next thing that happened really became the road to my demise. Don started telling me that he loved me --- just like I was --- fat or skinny. That is probably the worst thing that could have happened to me, because I truly believed him, and so we both started eating with reckless abandon. He was already putting his stamp of approval on my life-long overeating habit.

I dearly loved my freshman and sophomore years of high school, especially being in the band and being a part of the majorette line and representing my school. My favorite band director (I'm being factious here) pulled a surprise move for try-outs in the spring of 1971. Usually we tried out toward the end of the school year (May) – for the following year. Of course, I had put some weight back on, especially since Don and I loved to drive to Dallas to go out and eat. Also, we enjoyed going to sporting events, and that often meant a second dinner or snack on the way home. It could be a quick trip through Jack-In-The-Box for a couple of cheap tacos, on running into Lone Star Donuts at eleven o'clock at night for a dozen of hot, freshly-made donuts! Either way, I had been packing on the weight without really noticing it. I so thoroughly enjoyed my dating life with Don, but I didn't know that I had gotten so out of hand with the extra meals and unaccounted-for calories.

Unfortunately, I was a person that ate when I was happy. In fact, I also ate when I was sad, depressed, nervous, etc. Any little mood swing, kind of made me become like my alcoholic father. Eating always seemed to be my crutch – for whatever little bump in the road I came upon.

So, as I looked forward to my junior year, the band director had suddenly moved-up the try-out date a few months earlier than usual. Ott-O.....

Out of the blue, all the girls that had decided to try-out for majorette the following school year were asked to report to the band director's office after school. This was surprisingly in March of '71, even before Easter. So many of our older teammates were graduating that year in a couple of months, that it only left a few baton girls who wanted to or were qualified to try-out. Individually, he sent each one of us into another waiting room to be weighed. Of course, none of us thought he would actually weigh us that day, but he did it anyway.

Much to my chagrin, when it was my turn I stepped up on the scales and a nurse called out my weight of 157 pounds. According to the doctor's weight chart that she held in her hand, I was supposed to weight 130 to 135 pounds for my age and height. Back then, there were no variations based on the size of our frames, or any other contributing factors which might help or hurt the recording of my final weight. Basic hard fact: The nurse then broke my heart when she told me that I needed to lose a total of 22 pounds. Wow! I hadn't realized that I had gained that much weight, but there it was, written down in black and white.

After the band director enforced weigh-in, I realized my results weren't good. He called me aside and told me – one last time -- that according to his doctor's chart, I was 22 pounds overweight. He announced that I had two weeks to lose the weight, or I couldn't try-out. Now, keep in mind, that I was a State Champion twirler, had traveled all over the United States, and won all kinds of trophies, medals and titles. None of that mattered, at the moment.

The following is a current doctors' height and weight chart from 2014. Thankfully, things have generally changed for the better, at least where fat girls are concerned. Today's chart shows "Small Frame", "Medium Frame", and "Large Frame". So, in today's world, I would have only been a few pounds over the limit for a "large framed" high school girl.

Height And Weight Goals for Women			
Height	**Small Frame**	**Medium Frame**	**Large Frame**
4'10" 4'11" 5'0"	102-111 lbs. 103-113 104-115	109-121 lbs. 111-123 113-126	118-131 lbs. 120-134 112-137
5'1" 5'2" 5'3"	106-118 108-121 111-124	115-129 118-132 121-135	125-140 128-143 131-147
5'4" 5'5" 5'6"	114-127 117-130 120-133	124-141 127-141 130-144	137-151 137-155 140-159
5'7" 5'8" 5'9"	123-136 126-139 129-142	133-147 136-150 139-153	143-163 146-167 149-170
5'10" 5'11" 6'0"	132-145 135-148 138-151	142-156 145-159 148-162	152-176 155-176 158-179

I was in tears as I drug myself home and shared with my mother about the impossible task I had facing me. She jumped right in and told me that she would do anything she could to try and assist me. Short of praying for a miracle, I couldn't think of a thing she could do to help me at this juncture.

The next fourteen days were very tedious and hard to describe. I tried to eat very, very small meals, and followed each meal up with a half of grapefruit. I had successfully lost about 15 pounds in the same amount of time a couple of years ago, and by using the same grapefruit diet. You basically ate small amounts of protein at meal times and then the acid in the grapefruit that you added after the meal kind of ate-up the fat portion of the protein (like broiled steak, baked fish, etc.).

With only a couple of days left in the two-week period, I practically just tried starving myself. I felt really faint and was scared I might pass-out at school. That would have really embarrassed me, if they had had to call an ambulance to pick me up.

Anyway, I did the best I could. Everybody around me was trying to support me --- even my dad and Don, too. Try as I might, at the end of the two weeks, I was unable to reach the unattainable goal the band director had set for me. I was as low as I'd ever felt during my teenage years. I had lost 10 pounds by weigh-in day, but that still left me with 12 more to lose. That meant that I could not try-out for majorette for the following year (11th grade). No time extensions would be granted, which eliminated me from the opportunity to even try-out.

I was crushed beyond recognition. All of this happened on a Friday afternoon, and I had no desire to return to school on the following Monday. I played hooky and stayed at home a few days while I grieved for my place in life being snatched from me. I felt that my life was over.

Here I was, the reigning Amateur Athletic Union (A.A.U.) State Champion one and two baton twirler; I had traveled all over the country for lessons and camps and for various competitions. Individually, I had even competed at the National Baton Twirling Association's biggest event (N.B.T.A. "nationals") two different years in a row at St. Paul, Minnesota. Regardless of what any of us thought, because of twelve unwanted pounds, and as a result of the figures found on some stupid medical chart, I was booted out of my little high school majorette line.

I had never thought about suicide --- until now. This complete time of darkness was absolutely the lowest point of my young life thus far. I was so sick and disappointed that I wanted to take my own life. Here I was, a straight "A" student that now didn't want to even go back to school. But I kept hearing Jesus' words from the Bible, "I will never leave you nor forsake you." (Joshua 1:5)

My mother and father set up an appointment with my high school principal and the band director the following week to discuss me getting the old boot, but it really did no good. The band director wasn't budging, and the principal didn't have the guts to use his power and go over the head of the band director. You see, Mr. Band Director had been so successful with his band program at our school that no one dared try to oppose him in any way.

So, in a nutshell, this weight-prejudiced, narrow-minded band director (that vocally claimed to NOT like fat girls) single-handedly changed the course of my life. No longer did I really think about going to college (and I was ranked in the Top 10 of my 1973 Class). I probably could have gone to any of the major colleges on an academic or baton twirling scholarship, or both. But no longer did I feel the need to continue-on in baton twirling lessons and competitions, no longer did I care whether I was a part of my school or not. I didn't really care about any of it any more. I basically just wanted to get the heck out of there and graduate.

I immediately exited band class, and then the director had the audacity to send a note home to ask my mother why I had dropped out. My mother called and told him in no uncertain terms, "If you declared that Patty is too fat to twirl in front of your band, then she is certainly too fat to march and carry a horn in your organization."

Touché for my mother! She always stood beside me then, and she is still cheering me on as she looks down from heaven. She was my toughest critic and, also my biggest fan.

I had always wanted to be the first person in my family to attend college. Unfortunately, I let one man's opinion of me change my life's path, and it took me years to forgive him for how he damaged me by his decision.

In retrospect, we realized that what my parents should have done was to file a lawsuit against the school. But back then, no one really knew how to do just that. I guess it just makes me sick to my stomach when I go to high school football games today, and see so many overweight girls (and guys) in the drill teams, in the flag corps, in the bands, and even some in the cheerleading squads. Mostly I can't fathom it being "OK today" when I see 300-pound girls waving the large flags in front of their bands. It somehow doesn't seem fair to me. But on the other hand, I am so proud that they have the courage to be out in front of people at whatever size and it's great that they feel ok about themselves. I sometimes want to stand up in the stands and shout, "You go, Girl", or "You go, Boy"!

It reminds me of the movie, "An Officer and a Gentleman". One of the closing scenes is where Richard Geer comes into the factory and picks up his bride-to-be (Debra Winger), and carries her out in front of her girlfriend. This girlfriend is so proud for her. She certainly didn't get carried out of the "going-nowhere life", but her best friend did, so she was overjoyed at her friend's good fortune! That's how I feel when I see other overweight people getting recognition and acceptance these days. Maybe I wasn't accepted during my time in high school, but fat people do have rights today to be a part of things and to be a "real" person regardless of their size.

CHAPTER 9

Did Someone Say Wedding Bells?

Don and I became inseparable, especially after I had been shut out from being a majorette for the band. Before I knew it, I was in my junior year at Lancaster High. I had a promise ring from Don, was in possession of his football letter jacket, as well as his senior class ring. We were so wrapped-up in each other's lives, even in the smallest of details. I loved him, and he loved me, and nothing was going to break us up --- not even our parents. His mom and dad didn't think I was good enough for him, their only child. And my parents didn't think he was good enough for me either.

My mother convinced me to stay involved in some of the school clubs I was a part of, so I then encouraged Don to join me in some of my favorite after school activities. We were now both signed-up to be writers for our school newspaper. I was in "Future Teachers of America", so that meant that he also became part of my club. Both of us enjoyed being in the "Spanish Club" because the teacher seemed to be so dorky that we sat back and watched the mean boys trick him into all kinds of messes. We also went out to eat Mexican food from time to time as a club, so that was always a fun night of laughter and a way to enjoy each other's company, even in a group setting.

The school year of 1971-1972 flashed by so quickly that it was time for Don to graduate in late May. Who knew what changes that might bring to our relationship? He found a steady job right off the bat after graduation, so now he really wanted to spend his "own" money on me. He no longer had to beg his parents for cash; he had resources of his own.

We were getting along famously in the fall (1972) of my senior year. I went to school every day, and he went off to work. We were unable to see each other nearly as much as before, so we messed-up one night in late October. He stayed over at my house until about 2:00 in the morning. He tried to sneak-in his parents' house, but his dad caught him red-handed. He gave him the old song-and-dance about Don having to follow his rules as long as he was living under his father's roof.

Don tried to tell him that he was now out of school, and he shouldn't have to have a set curfew at almost 19 years of age. He also admitted to his dad that he could move out if need be, so there would be no more problem of him living under his father's roof. The whole ugly confrontation turned into an all-out war between himself and his parents. They grounded him and told him that he couldn't see me for two weeks. His parents called my mom and announced that both of us had broken our curfews. But when you're young and in love, two weeks of grounding can seem like a lifetime. Both of us were so upset and mad at our parents that we devised a secret plan of our own. In our inexperienced, little, adolescent minds, we would get back at them. Just wait and see......

This was the final straw for our relationship. I didn't want to wait any longer to marry the love of my life, Don Hullett. I think the big factors in my decision were (1) the grounding by our parents; (2) the majorette disappointment; and (3) that I wanted to get out of my parents' house of turmoil. I was pretty much done with all the fussing and fighting.

One of our very favorite teachers in our high school was the man that taught seniors the required "Government" class. He was so totally cool and all the kids loved him. He was the kind of guy that was more like a counselor, he had a keen ear for listening, and all the kids seemed to love him. Almost any student could feel comfortable coming to him with a problem or for advice. After our ridiculous grounding, that kind of gave me an open invitation to ask Mr. Government some pertinent questions about Don and I running off and getting married without our parents' permission.

As he explained it to me, we could travel across the state border to Oklahoma, and their legal age limit for marriage was only eighteen. That would work for us, as I had just turned eighteen in September of 1972.

It appeared that we could get married without our parents even knowing about it. What a great teacher! (The ironic thing is that the same Mr. Government was my oldest daughter's Government teacher when she was a senior at our same high school. However, I had already contacted him and let him know that if he ever helped MY daughter run away and get married, that I would kill him! He laughed, but I think he knew that I meant it!)

So, we began to set our plan in motion. We spent our evenings on the telephone, plotting our escape. A few of our friends knew about it, but not that many. Our grand scheme was to take place around Thanksgiving when I would have a few days off from school because of the holiday. We were always let-out early on the Wednesday afternoon before Turkey Day. It was our intent for Don to pick me up from school, we would drive to Oklahoma City, stay in a hotel for a couple of nights, and then we'd get married at the courthouse on Friday. That would give us a few days of a honeymoon, and then I could be back at school on time on Monday morning. The plan was set, and it was almost T-minus countdown, when someone foiled our air-tight arrangement for our almost secret elopement!

I think one of our mutual friends was a cousin to one of Don's cousins --- but Don and the girl were not really related themselves. She went home and leaked our news the weekend before our planned departure. She told her mom, her mom got on the phone and told the cousin's mom, then this lady (Don's aunt --- his mother's sister) called his mom --- and the plan was smashed to pieces. (This kin folk stuff was very confusing to me, also.). All I know, was that everything we had envisioned, didn't come together because someone couldn't keep their mouth shut.

You must remember that we are talking about the year of 1972. Back then, no one intentionally talked out-loud about someone getting pregnant out of wedlock. It was a hush-hush kind of thing. Well, this saga really didn't occur to me until years later, but I think both sets of parents were so closed-mouthed about us wanting to run off and get married, that no one took the time to ask us if we were pregnant or not. There was no pregnancy going on here. We were both just mad at our parents and wanted to get married, come hell or high water!

My mother begged me not to marry Don. She even promised that she would buy me any new car (or any other worldly possession) that I wanted, if I would just not marry him. His parents did practically the same thing to him, offering him a car or money if he would agree to change his mind. It was just not happening. We were both stubborn and in love, so neither of us came off the promise we had made to each other to get married over that Thanksgiving weekend.

Through all the turmoil and stress during my senior year of high school, I continued to battle my growing weight problem and my weird, inner voices. In fact, a few days before my wedding ceremony I encountered one of those very hurtful "fat moments". If you've ever had a weight problem or had a loved one that is overweight, then you might understand what I mean. During my lifetime, I have endured many, many fat stories that could have resulted in making or breaking me. I am confident, however, that in the midst of these uncomfortable instances, I feel I rose above the pain and indignation the majority of the time.

My mother and I only had a couple of days to put together an impromptu wedding, of sorts. We didn't have the money or extra time to shop for a real bridal gown, so we opted to try a couple of well-known department stores to find an appropriate, ready-made, wedding dress that way. I tried on about ten different long gowns, but I finally chose one that was very lacy, off-white in color, with an empire-style waist, a ruffle that circled my scoop-neck bodice, and a large ruffle around the bottom of the floor-length dress. To me, it was just perfect.

My mother seemed to approve of the "off-white" color saying that it would be the "approved" color for "my" situation. I didn't get her meaning at the time. That's how naïve I was at age eighteen. With that comment, what my mother was implying was that I should not get married in "white", because I was pregnant. To her, "off-white" would be the acceptable choice of color.

I then took my perfect dress home and tried it on for my sister to see. She liked it, too, but I noticed when I tried it on at home, that part of the long ruffle at the bottom of the dress had not been sewn properly. The seamstress must have missed part of the ruffle on the sewing machine. It was like approximately two or three inches of the ruffle had not been properly attached. That meant that I had to take the dress back to the department store the following day. They would either need to have the dress altered, or they would have to provide a replacement dress.

I was so proud of my new dress when I walked up to the "Special Occasion Dresses" area of the store and plopped my size 20 dress on the counter. A sales clerk finally strolled over to the cash register, raised-up some of the material, then rudely told me that I needed to take my curtains back to the drapery department for my return or refund.

It caught me off-guard for a few seconds, but when I finally got my voice back, I quietly set her straight by saying, "This is my wedding dress, not a pair of lacy curtains."

In turn, she replied, "Well, I thought it was curtains because there were yards and yards of material piled-up on the counter."

"OUCH"! Have you felt that someone just slapped you in the face, without really slapping you? Well, that was exactly how I felt. I was cut down to size with one rude, insensitive sentence.

I tried to pick-up my crushed ego, and my new replacement dress, and headed out of the store. After all, we still had to pick out flowers, rings, my bouquet, etc. There was absolutely no time for hurt feelings or for crying all the way home. But I cried anyway.

So, with only one day before Wednesday, our M-Day ("marriage" day), we worked out with my grandmother's church that her preacher would marry us before their Wednesday night prayer service. They basically were whisking us in and whisking us out, in about a 30-minute time span.

It was a very small wedding, only a few of our close friends and sorted family members were there. Before the service began, the preacher had talked to Don and told him it would be ok if he wanted to run out the back door – that he still had time. In that instant, he said he thought of the part of the vows stating "until death do us part", so he said that sealed it for him. There was no turning back now.

On the very first step that my father and I took as we started down the middle aisle of the church, I tripped on the hem of my perfect dress. Next, my very best girlfriend, Mary, was scheduled to stand up with me during the marriage vows, but she had somehow gotten lost and had trouble finding the church. She didn't make it until the service had already started. So, my sister, who I am not very close to at all, ended up being my "Maid of Honor". Don's best friend did not show-up at all, so another guy, someone Don really didn't know very well, stood in as his "Best Man". Call it foreboding, but the wedding didn't seem to be starting off on the right foot.

The poor preacher did his best, but it was extremely hard for everybody there to concentrate, especially since Don's mother and my father were crying so loudly that no one could hear the vows. We somehow muddled through, and we became "man and wife", despite our parents' disdain.

Don always jokingly reminds our friends that two terrible things happened on November 22nd. President John F. Kennedy was assassinated on the streets of Dallas in 1963, and Don and Patty got married nine years later (1972) on the same ominous date.

It was a very uncomfortable feeling walking back into my high school classes the following Monday as a married woman. Some of the guys gave me the dreaded "wink", letting me know that they knew exactly what I had been up to over the Thanksgiving holidays! Most of my girlfriends were very supportive of me. In fact, a lot of them thought our spoiled "get-away, gone wrong" was very romantic, even though we had to end up getting married in our small-town USA.

So, my senior year moved on, with me being a very busy student. I was now entering a new chapter of my life, being a "wife" to my high school sweetheart. We married and then moved into an apartment of our own in the center of our city. There were no parental curfews for us to worry about any longer......

CHAPTER 10

Welcome to Adulthood,
a/k/a The Rat Race

In the 70s there were only a few choices for <u>women</u> in the business world. I could be a school teacher, but scratch that one --- no college. Or, I could be a nurse, but scratch that one, too --- the no college thing reared its ugly ahead again. Or, I could be a secretary. It seemed the logical choice for me, especially since I had taken a secretarial class each year during high school – Typing 1, Shorthand, Typing 2, and Clerical Practice. My last four years in high school should have counted for something. Surely, I had acquired enough office skills that I could find a secretarial job and make a decent living using this occupational choice. (By the way, the other female choice for work was to be a homemaker or a stay-at-home mom. Neither of those choices appealed to me at the time, especially since other people seemed to still think I was pregnant.)

Since I had shelved my life-long dream of going to college and married instead, I had very few options for my career path. I graduated in late May of 1973. No counselor ever called me in his/her office to even talk about the possibility of me going on to college. In looking back, I now realize that most everyone in my school (including the faculty) must have thought that I "had" to get married. Not one teacher or counselor or school staff member ever approached me at all. With no real encouragement from my parents (Don and I had made our own bed, now we had to lie in it) and no support from my school, I entered the work force. I graduated on a Thursday evening, and started my first job on the following Monday at an insurance company in downtown Dallas.

Welcome to the "Rat Race", Patty. Is adulthood all that you thought it would be?

Note to Self: 1ST ADULT OBSERVATION – Maybe our parents knew a little bit about what they were trying to tell us about the necessity of going to college.

Regardless, I liked my first job ok. It was a clerical entry-level position, so it was definitely easy enough for me to do well at. The company was in the heart of the city, so that was a neat plus. In fact, it was very cool to walk downstairs to cash my paycheck each Friday. Then, I could trek on down the street, and spend some of my hard-earned money at some of the lush department stores nearby. The disappointment came when I would try clothing on, and either it wouldn't fit me, or it looked totally awful on my continually growing body. By this time, I was wearing a size 22 or 24, and I weighed over 200 pounds. It was certainly nothing at all to be proud of.

I guess Don and I were making it ok as a newlywed couple. I wasn't a great cook, but I was learning. My mother was always just a quick telephone call away to help me. We even made some friends in our apartment complex, so we had a few couples to run around with.

We spent a lot of our extra time with Don playing in men's softball leagues. That kept us frantically busy almost every weeknight. He was getting plenty of exercise, but I was not, just sitting on the bleachers. It seemed like I just kept gaining more and more weight, and all the while, feeling worse about myself. I had become more introverted, not the usual outgoing person I was back in school.

It didn't help when negative things started happening to me either. I'd be pushing my full grocery basket back to the car, and I'd hear some young guys saying something like, "Look at the Fatso emptying the shelves at the Food Mart". I would try to pretend that I didn't hear their rude comments, but it would break my heart on the inside. It got to where I became paranoid about being seen in public.

Sometimes I would get called into my doctor's office for a general checkup, and I felt like all eyes were staring at me when I'd cross the room for my exam. I'd always want to turn back around to all the people starring and say, "Haven't you ever seen a fat lady before?" Another time, I remember falling as I started up our stairs at our apartment, and several young men standing around their cars started laughing at me. None of these things did anything but make me feel more terrible about myself.

I did well at my first job at the insurance company. Unfortunately, they discovered my aptitude for math, so they had me figuring premiums and that sort of thing. I didn't really like mathematics all that much, so I quit after about a year of working in the insurance world.

I decided to follow in my mother's footsteps at her one-and-only real job, Sears and Roebuck & Company, the catalog division. I was so excited that I was about to become an employee in their "Customer Relations / Correspondence" (and "Complaints") department. In the back of my brain I was thinking......... "If I could only work my way up to become a correspondent (or letter-writer), then maybe I would be able to use my writing skills."

I literally had to start at the bottom of the rung at the Sears ladder of success. I began my career there as a mail station clerk, and then made my way on up to a runner/messenger for the department. Both were boring jobs, but at least I got the chance to walk around in the large buildings which spread over about two city blocks. I enjoyed lots of good exercise and that kept my mind occupied, too.

I next moved-up to a desk called "Due Us". This was a mundane and useless position where Sears customers didn't quite pay their monthly bill in their entirety --- in all cases the amount "Due Us" was under $5.00. In fact, I thought it was simply ridiculous that often I would mail-out a form letter month after month in the effort to collect something like (i.e.) "two bucks". After few months with no response, Sears had ultimately spent much more money and man power to collect the "two bucks" than was feasible in the grand scheme of things in the accounting world. But it was a job, and I somewhat enjoyed it.

On down the road I was elated to see that the time had come for me to move into a "Junior Correspondent" position. The excitement didn't last very long, however, as I then realized that I still would not be writing my own "special" letters. In almost every circumstance, each correspondent

selected a "form letter" to answer the customer's complaint and/or concern. I generally just selected the correct form letter and then signed my name before mailing the correspondence out. Can anyone spell ----
B-O-R-E-D-O-M ????

The one thing that I did enjoy at Sears was the hysterical letters that customers would send in to gripe or complain. Most of the time, they were writing to ask for a refund for a product they thought didn't live-out its length-of-use expectancy. The correspondents often would share some of the very best humorous and/or outlandish letters with the office co-workers. That way, we all got to enjoy the laughs at the expense of some of Sears' craziest customers.

I remember a cool story about a man's car catching on fire and it being destroyed, and it burned to the ground. Interestingly enough, the guy took the trouble to write Sears and tell them that their "Die Hard" battery was the best thing on earth. The very satisfied customer told our Correspondence Department that the battery was removed from the totaled automobile, but the man proudly explained how he cleaned it up, installed it on another car, and the battery fired-up immediately, without a hint of hesitation! Well-pleased customers were not usually the "norm".

Another funny instance, was when an elderly lady wrote in and complained about her girdle not holding-in her stomach any longer, and she was most definitely not happy. In this incidence, the correspondent simply picked up the phone, dialed the woman's phone number, and ask her, point-blank, how long she had owned the Sears brand girdle. The disappointed customer then proudly replied, "I've had this girdle for over fifteen years, and I want my money back". The employee quickly finished the call and returned the receiver to its carrier on the phone set. After she had time to stop laughing, she did what any good Sears customer service person used to do (back in "the day"). She OK'd a "half" refund, even though the worn-out girdle's life expectancy should have been about five years. No wonder why Sears' success has greatly declined in the past few decades --- because they were a little "too" forgiving and afraid to say "no" to their customers --- even when a refund was not warranted or expected.

My mother thought that Sears was the only real place on earth to work, as in the end, she worked for almost forty years there as an employee of that company. However, as a youngster in my early twenties, Sears was not the place or answer for me. I tried to change gears and see what other kind of office job I could come up with. But bear in mind that this was in the mid-seventies and I was a very overweight young woman. I perused the Dallas local newspapers and tried to answer any interesting secretarial jobs that I thought I would be qualified for, but finding any type of job turned-out to be challenging for me as a fat person.

One morning I answered a "want ad" and finally got to speak directly to one of the attorneys at a prestigious law firm in downtown Dallas. The man seemed to be impressed with my good telephone voice and past work experience --- or at least he was impressed with me over the phone. I was excited because this was a front office (or in other words, a receptionist/ secretary) position that I was trying to obtain. I was instructed to come to Dallas in the afternoon for a personal interview, and if everything looked ok, I could probably start to work for them on the following Monday.

When the "temp" receptionist called me into the attorney's office, I could see the shocking disappointment on his face. I was qualified --- but I was overweight and not what he had in mind to represent his law firm in the reception area. He went through a very condensed interview process, and then told me that he had come across some other job candidates after he had spoken to me earlier in the morning. So instead of him telling me that I had the job and could start on Monday, his response now became.......
"We'll give you a call back in a few days" --- which meant that I would not hear back from him at all, and that is exactly what happened. I had the job until the man saw that I was overweight. I could read the rejection in his eyes. And I can't tell you how many times the same scenario played out for me because of my handicap of being morbidly obese.

Not giving up, a few weeks later I read another "want ad" that sounded like interesting work. It was a secretarial position for "The Dallas Lighthouse for the Blind". Now, I felt like I was getting somewhere. The ad divulged the fact that their successful candidate would be working for two bosses that were totally blind. That should work out well, because the blind people certainly couldn't be prejudiced against folks that were fat. They would not be able to visually "see" that I was overweight. So, I quickly called the listed phone number and set up an interview which was to happen in a couple of days.

I was so impressed when I sat down in their reception area and saw a totally blind person answering their busy phones. This receptionist was aptly able to field each call by using some sort of electronic pen device that could tell which button had the active call to be answered. I was so inspired by the technology and expertise of this blind employee at The Dallas Lighthouse for the Blind.

A few minutes later I was ushered down the long hallway to the first boss' office. The lady seemed very nice and we talked for several minutes about my work background and office skills. The lady also had a guide dog, a large German shepherd next to her desk. that she had lying near her feet. When we completed our conversation, she had her dog lead us gingerly down the hall again to a different office. The older gentleman introduced himself and started asking me questions as part of my interview process. Suddenly, he paused and asked me a weird question that I didn't see coming. He very directly asked me if I was overweight. Stunned at his boldness, I quietly answered "yes". He proceeded to explain that he could tell I was overweight because of my heavy breathing that he picked-up on, because of his keen sense of hearing.

And then it happened to me again. No return phone call, and probably another good job lost because of my fatness. I know now that even blind people can "sense" my handicap of being overweight, and I suppose that they didn't want me to work for them either. Another rude case of size discrimination again!

After several more negative job interviews, I ascertained that I was being stereo-typed as a "fat" person. In a lot of people's minds "fat" meant "slow" and/or "lazy". I seriously hated that connotation and everything that went along with that implication. I was never lazy, and I still am not. I can attest to the fact that much of my young married years were spent working a regular 40-hour job, as well as other side occupations in my spare time. I was like the Energizer Bunny on the battery commercial. No matter what happened in my life, I was constantly working and in motion. Anyone who really knew me would testify that I was never slow or lazy. And I was ready to fight anyone that thought otherwise of me.

Some of these hurtful experiences caused me to somewhat develop an attitude of carrying-around a chip on my shoulder. I had been disappointed and crushed so many times because of my appearance. It seemed so terribly unfair to me.

On down the road, I seemed to fit much better into a mostly-women workplace, especially since a lot of the ladies were overweight like me. In fact, we chitchatted during our breaks about all our weight-loss woes. We formed what we termed the "B.O.B." Club. And in case you're wondering....... Of course, the initials stood for "Big Old Butts" ("B.O.B.") Club. I felt very comfortable and at-ease in a friendlier environment which included so many others experiencing the same kind of injustice as me. You know the old saying....... "The (fat) birds of a feather flock together."

I was now almost 21 years old when Don and I decided that we might want to have a child of our own. It seemed like all the couples that we ran with already had small children. The others were a couple of years older than us, but we didn't care. We had been married for over two years, so we decided to go for it.

The process didn't take but a few short weeks, and, bam, I was expecting. It had never occurred to me that a gynecologist would have strict rules about how much weight I could gain during my pregnancy, especially since he determined that I was a little overweight to be having a baby in the first place. He warned that gaining more weight could be a health hazard to both me and the unborn child.

I was very careful about what I ate, and I even lost a few pounds in my first couple of months. Everything seemed to be running along very smoothly. I was very proud to be pregnant, because in my head, I thought I had a valid reason to "look" fat. I wanted to wear cute maternity clothes, right off the bat. However, I realized that wasn't going to be happening, since there were very few maternity clothes that came in my size, 22 or 24, and later on, size 26, as my tummy got bigger.

I basically had to go with bigger, "old lady" clothes. That was what I called them, and they were not very attractive at all. Back then, the sonograms were not very trusting, and with me being so thick-bodied, the doctor really couldn't get a true reading when I periodically went for a sonogram. In the last trimester, the doctor couldn't even hear a heartbeat for the baby.

When I was two or three weeks away from my scheduled due date, the doctor thought the fetus might be stillborn, because he could detect no heartbeat at all. Don and I were devastated, but I was encouraged to carry-on to full-term and we'd have to wait and see what happened then.

I had only gained about ten pounds the first eight months, so I was super-proud of myself. However, I was so nervous about the possibility of delivering a stillborn baby, that I really kicked my old eating habits into gear. As I said before, when I was nervous, I did the only thing that came natural to me. Yes, and the more nervous I got, the more I ate.

In fact, during the day of December 3, 1974, I had baked a batch of chocolate chip cookies and I had eaten every single one by myself! I felt so bloated and guilty about what I'd done that day, and I couldn't really sleep. I just kept tossing and turning and began to feel constipated. After a few hours after midnight, I finally realized that this constipation feeling might truly be labor pains. Don then talked me into calling my doctor in the middle of the night, but his sweet wife told me that it was probably nothing, and that I should take a couple of aspirin and try to go back to sleep. I waited a couple more hours and phoned my doctor again, at about daybreak. Sure enough, the doctor himself told me to get myself on to the hospital and he would meet me there.

I went through about twenty hours of labor. I had no idea of how much time had gone by, but more and more women would join me in the birthing area. It seemed like each one would scream and wail, their baby would be born, and then they would be ushered out of the area, only to be moved upstairs to their own private room. That is, everybody but me. I was aware of an endless stream of women coming in and going out of the birthing area. I seemed to be a permanent resident there.

Finally, my doctor determined that my labor pains didn't seem to be coming close enough together, so he would have to do a C-section on me. That was perfectly fine with me. Just put me to sleep, and let me get this thing over with, please. I braced myself for whatever might be coming my way, but when I woke up in the recovery room a few hours later, I was the mother of a 9-pound, 10 ounce bouncing baby girl. There was not a thing in the world wrong with her.

The doc determined that I was just so thick that the sonogram equipment did not properly pick up the perfectly fine heartbeat of my new big baby. And when they weighed me coming into the hospital, (even after eating all the freshly baked cookies), I had only gained twelve pounds during my entire nine-month pregnancy. I was quite pleased with myself, and I considered this a victory for me and my healthy baby girl.

CHAPTER 11

What a Catch

I promised myself that I would do everything in my power to keep from naming my new baby anything that rhymed with "fat". I had envisioned her being a "Heather", especially since I thought "Heather Hullett" sounded like a movie star's name. However, after Don and I gazed upon our new creation, "Heather" just didn't seem to fit her. Also, I had numerous other girlfriends that had already or would be soon naming their little darlings "Heather" as well. Thus, cross-out the name of "Heather", and enter the name that my mother suggested ---- "Buffy". She had come up with that name, based on the seventies TV show called "Family Affair". In this 30-minute sit-com, Uncle Bill, a bachelor, was raising his nieces and nephew, Cissy, Buffy and Jody.

Everybody was enthralled with the cutesy name of "Buffy", so that's what we decided to go with. The real problem was trying to find a middle name that sounded good after "Buffy". I skimmed through a lot of baby books until I found the name of "Dionne" --- like the singing star Dionne Warwick. Everything now settled, our Buffy Dionne Hullett was officially named, and we went home to go about the task of becoming a real family.

I had gone through almost nine full months of morning sickness during my pregnancy, and sometimes I even had night sickness, too. A couple of weeks after coming home with the baby, I seemed to be continuing the practice of regularly throwing-up after most meals. As I had mentioned previously, I had only gained twelve pounds during the entire pregnancy, but the cool thing was that they weighed me at the hospital after giving birth, and I had immediately dropped about 35 pounds. I was ecstatic over the welcomed and surprising weight-loss. My OB-GYN promptly gave me a couple of prescriptions for "here we go again" diet pills. I tried them for about a week, and then Don flushed them down the toilet. He hated the way I acted while under their influence, and he said that he would rather me be as big as the side of a barn, rather than what the diet pills were turning me into.

However, I was still deeply puzzled as to why I kept throwing-up. Finally, I started having terrible abdominal pains late at night – after I would go to bed. Some of these pains (or cramps) were so excruciating that I woke Don up one night and told him to get a gun and shoot me. I stated that "death would be better than going through all of this pain". So, in thinking back, my labor pains seemed to be very minimal to me now, as compared to the extreme pain I was presently feeling.

Don called my clinic the next morning and got me an appointment with my OB-GYN doctor for a check-up. I asked the doctor, "Can you tell me why I'm still having morning sickness?" After a couple of quick tests, he told me the reason. No post-partum effects were to blame. What I had was a gall bladder full of gall stones. So, that was probably the real reason I had suffered so horribly with the morning/evening sickness when I was pregnant. My doctor sent me straight on to a gastro specialist, and I was admitted to the hospital the very next day.

Now, not only did I have the long incision and painful C-section staples to handle, I also had a gall bladder incision and drain opening after the successful gall bladder surgery. And afterwards, the funny thing was that the surgeon told me that I was not to lift more than ten pounds. Well, our baby girl was already over that milestone, so how could a new mother not pick up her newborn child? It was very trying to keep from holding my baby, but I tried to follow the doctor's orders as best I could. We even had a family relative stay with us for a few days to help me with taking care of Buffy, since I wasn't allowed to pick her up or hold her.

After a few more weeks of healing, we traveled back to the surgeon's office to have the stitches removed and everything seemed fine. On the way home, we stopped at the grocery store to pick up a few things. As we moved up and down the aisles, we became keenly aware of a terrible odor. Both of us thought it was the homeless-looking lady that had passed us on one of the aisles.

Finally, Don asked me, "What is that horrible smell?" I retorted, "I have no idea, but it is awful." About that time, I felt fluid running down one of my legs. Back to the doctor's office we went at a high rate of speed. I had realized that my gall bladder incision had ruptured!

The doctor fixed me up again, cleaned out the oozing incision, and sent me back home to recuperate another couple of weeks. About this time, Don had bought our first boat, and we had named her appropriately, "The Buffy D". Don's parents had a weekend get-away place down at the lake, about an hour from where we lived. We couldn't wait for me to heal, so we could take our boat to the lake and try it out.

The boat was awesome. We loved going down to the lake every weekend. None of us could really ski. I had tried that previously and failed miserably. Don kiddingly kept telling me that he needed a much bigger boat if he was going to get my big derriere out of the water. Regardless, we loved riding in our little blue and white boat. Sometimes we even did some fishing.

One weekend, we shook-up our routine and asked some of our friends, Gary and Sharon, to join us at a closer lake to home. They consented to take us up on our offer. We took along a picnic lunch and headed to our afternoon destination. We spent a couple of hours boat-riding, and then we docked for a while to stop and eat our lunch. As we headed back across the lake, Don and Gary decided to stop the boat, and jump in for some swimming to cool-off. I really hadn't planned to get in the water, but it was so darn hot that summer day in the Texas heat, that Sharon and I jumped in as well.

We splashed, floated, and swam around the boat area for about forty-five minutes. Exhausted, we then started climbing aboard again, one-by-one, so we could head for home. Well, Gary jumped up onto the side of the boat first, pulled himself in, and then turned to give Don a boost. Sharon was tall and feather-light, so she was no problem at all to get inside the boat.

Keeping in mind that I had gone through two major surgeries within a six-week period, and also knowing that I was still very overweight, I had another rough obstacle to face. Try as I might, I could not possibly pull myself far enough on the side of the boat for the guys to pull me in. As soon as I'd get myself on the boat's wall, I would have to let go because of the pain I was experiencing from the two still tender scar areas (both on my mid-section). The fellows tried for about thirty minutes to help lift me into the boat, but it was just not happening. After a while I started to cry and told them to just leave me there to die. I confessed that I was just too big to get back into the boat. And I also felt totally degraded in front of our friends. I was embarrassed, and they were embarrassed for me.

Finally, Don improvised a plan to get me to the lake's shore. He would use the ski rope and tow me to the beach area. I didn't want to follow his plan, but I couldn't think of anything better for us to try. Can you imagine what the people thought when Don came as close to the beach as possible towing his extra-large wife at the end of the ski rope? It was so painful watching the faces of the people as I walked myself up on the beach. All I could think was, they were probably saying to themselves, "Wow. He caught a whale out there today. And she must already be trained. She can even walk herself onto the shore." I felt as if I was experiencing a whole new level of loss of self-respect. It was not a good feeling at all. And there, in that moment, I made a promise to myself to never jump into the water from a boat, no matter how hot the temperature might be.

CHAPTER 12

History Repeats Itself

When Buffy was born she came out with a head full of hair. To us, she looked like a little doll. She was impishly cute and quite the charmer. Don and I were so proud of her and all the adorable things she could do. As a toddler, she loved to stand in front of the TV and watch "Happy Days". And, of course, her favorite actor was Henry Winkler, "The Fonz". In fact, her first real word (if you can call it that) was "Ayyyyyyyy", what Fonzie said on the show all the time. We proudly would ask her, "What does Fonzie say", and she would reply in her best voice, "Ayyyyyyyy".

Later, we were so thrilled when she started saying words, like "yes", "no", and "mama" -- but no "daddy" or "dada". She seemed to really have trouble trying to figure out WHAT to call Don. (A lot of people have trouble with trying to put a proper name on him, too!) Anyway, Buffy finally came up with "Dida". That was his father and grandpa name from then on. All the kids in our family today still call him "Dida".

I think some of my father must have rubbed off on me, because I liked to call Buffy a lot of other little nicknames, "silly" names at that. Don and I had come up with "Buff-Buff", "Boo", "Chewy" (or "Chewbacca" -- like the Wookie from "Star Wars"), and our personal favorite, "Too-E".

We thought we had the smartest kid ever, when we would show Buffy off in front of our family and friends by asking her name. We would challenge her, "So what is your real name? She would quickly answer, "Buffy".

Next, we would ask her, "And what does your Mama and Dida **call** you?" She would wrinkle-up her cute little face and reply, "Toooooo – E". It was just the most adorable thing ever.

Like mother, like daughter, Buffy was a chubby little thing. She was a sweetheart, but with lots of baby fat still left on her by the time school started. She did fine in our church's kindergarten program, but the real test seemed to take place in the first grade of public school. She had only been in her all-day classes for a couple of weeks when she came home upset about what some of the kids were calling her. Thank goodness, it could not possibly be "Fatty Patty" like the name that I had endured my entire childhood. But instead, they were quite creative and they came up with "Stuffy Buffy" and "Buff Buffalo". Here's so much for me figuring out an un-rhyming first name! The fact remains today, that kids will always be kids. And if they choose to make fun of or ridicule others, they can somehow find or create a way to do it.

Per Dr. James C. Dobson, author of the 1999 book *"The New Hide or Seek"*..........

"Children are destructive to the weak and lowly because we adults haven't bothered to teach them to FEEL for one another."

The one, good, positive thing that seemed to be motivating to Buffy was playing sports. She learned early-on that excelling in a sport made her feel good about herself!

To start off her career, she came home in the first grade with a registration form to sign up to participate in city-league soccer. Don and I were always such sports fanatics anyway, that we consented for her to give soccer a try. Don admitted that he knew very little about soccer, but she could give it a go anyway.

We religiously took Buffy to her bi-weekly soccer practices, but it didn't seem to be doing any good. The lady coach knew absolutely zero about soccer. In fact, she spent most of her time coaching from her car. She would have the kids get in a big circle and just kick the soccer ball back and forth, to each other. No wonder they got beat in their first game fifteen to nothing! The little girls were all so thoroughly confused, as they kept waiting to see when they would get in the big circle, like they spent their time doing in their regular practice sessions.

After a few games of getting killed by the teams from other towns, Don asked the lady coach if she could use a little help. Well, that was all it took, and within a couple of weeks, Don took over the squad completely and learned the game of soccer as the season went along. Now Buffy's team was at least scoring a few goals and Buffy really liked playing goalie. They weren't really winning any games, but with Coach Don they at least were beginning to become competitive. And Buffy enjoyed being the hero of the game. She loved how the crowd would cheer when she would make a great save in goal.

The next soccer season Don had successfully broken away from the city club soccer, and they became an independent soccer team for girls "Under 8". The "Orange Crush" came into existence, and the girls started winning a few games for a change. And Buffy had really blossomed into an awesome goalkeeper.

About this time, our second daughter was born and we became a two-daughter family. The girls were almost five years apart. Amber Dawn Hullett seemed to break the "fat baby" mold of our family, as she weighed-in at a normal birth weight of just over seven pounds. She certainly didn't command all the attention like Buffy did, so she was often a "background" kind of kid. In fact, as a toddler, Don would be coaching Buffy's soccer team, I would be keeping up with the stats of the game, and we'd look up and realize that we had forgotten we had a second child to watch over. We would find little Amber under the bleachers, or even one day down the road from the soccer fields, very near a horse grazing along the fence line.

Wow! That was a very important wake-up call. She could have gotten kicked in the head if we hadn't found her in time. Amber was a cute little thing, too, but because Buffy chose to play soccer and softball, we favored her because of her sports abilities. I'm not saying that was a good thing, but that's just how Don and I approached our two very different daughters.

Buffy became an incredible athlete, and was above-average at slow-pitch softball, too. She was so big and hefty that she could pound the ball unlike any other 7, 8, 9 or 10-year-old female in her league. She was extremely rough and tough, so much so that most girls her age were simply afraid of her. When she came up to bat, everybody on the field backed up. No one wanted to get creamed with a line drive off the bat of Buffy Hullett. She was also known as the "Homerun Hitting Queen". And with her being so chunky, you can imagine how far she must have been able to hit the ball, because she had to make it around all four bases, and fast running was not her strong suit. Hitting the ball, a long, long way, was.

In the sports arena, I don't remember Buffy getting kidded too often, mainly because I think both the girls and boys were either in awe of or scared of her. She was big and athletic, and everybody knew who she was. And the good thing about being named "Buffy" was that people always remembered her name.

It was time for Buffy to change gears in her sports personality at about age 11 or 12. She became more and more interested in playing her new sport of basketball as she approached her years in junior high school. She seemed to have a knack for shooting hoops, especially the 3-point variety. As a result, her dad came to her rescue again and decided that he would coach a youth league basketball team for girls in her age group. She was enthralled with playing recreational ball, but when she got to the point of joining her 7th and 8th grade school teams, it was entirely a different story.

Buffy was part of a huge successful junior high program, and each year they had 50 to 60 girls that ALL wanted very badly to play basketball. I can still visualize her perched at the end of the bench, sitting as close as possible to her very obese lady coach. Buffy thought that this situation might play right into her hand, as surely the overweight lady would be able to muster some sentiment and empathy for another fat person like herself.

Some games I would watch Buffy literally stare at this coach, just begging with her puppy-dog eyes saying, "Pick me, pick me, please pick me to go into the game. Please just give me one little chance."

But the lady rarely even let her leave her permanent spot on the bench. A genuine playing opportunity never really presented itself to Buffy. No matter how hard she hustled in practice and shot hoops in her spare time at home, she never really got the chance in junior high for her to prove her worth as a contributor to the team. There were so many cheerleaders that also participated in the basketball program, that we felt the overweight coach enjoyed getting to be best buds with the cute little cheerleader types. Buffy was definitely not cut-out to be a cheerleader, so she never merited the happenstance of the prejudiced lady coach.

After that, we even moved our family back to our smaller home town in hopes that Buffy would have a better shot at playing varsity sports. In the summer before her entering the 9th grade in high school, she became aware of the major problem she might face in making the high school basketball team. She ultimately realized that her weight might be one of the roadblocks she was experiencing in her attempt to become a starter. Having been down that same road a few times myself, I suddenly came up with a plan for Buffy to lose weight, and to lose it very quickly.

Just in time before she was to enter high school, I improvised a déjà vu experience from my past, to aid my daughter in making the ball team. I tracked-down and found the very same quack doctor that had supplied me with the high-powered amphetamine pills when I was in the fifth grade.

Buffy and I went to her first appointment, and this was not an easy thing for me to do. All I remembered about this doctor was that he made me feel terrible about myself. When he looked at me as a child, it was as if he detested fat people in general. In my mind's eye, I recalled that it seemed like it kind of made him sick to make direct eye contact with his overweight patient (like me), so none of my ugly fat might attach itself to his perfectly skinny frame. To me, he was a breathing, living oxymoron --- a person that couldn't stand looking at a fat person without getting physically sick to his stomach. But, at the same time, he certainly did not flinch one bit about taking the green money from all his obese patients and/or their desperate parents.

As fate would play out, it didn't take long before Buffy and I entered the office of Doctor "I Hate Fat People". He had his nurse weigh Buffy, and then asked her some personal questions about her life and background. While he was looking over his notes, I tried to interact with this "good doctor". I proudly announced to him that I used to be one of his patients when I was a little younger than Buffy's age, and that he had helped me lose 30 or 40 pounds back years ago. With that, he raised up his little rude head, and with his very meanest face he retorted in a matter-of-factly kind of way, "Sorry lady, but it's apparent that nothing has ever helped you"!

This cruel old coot had delivered yet another low blow to me and my ego. Bewildered by his curt comment, we completed Buffy's appointment and we left his office, with my "fat" tail tucked between my "overly-obese" legs. He had to be the most impolite doctor ever, and he had zero bedside manner about himself at all. I told Don that he would be in-charge of taking

Buffy to her upcoming doctor appointments in the future. I had determined that I was totally done with this jackass of a doctor.

The astounding thing was that Buffy had never really dieted her whole life, but she had quickly lost about 25 pounds just before she began the 9th grade. Everything started off very well, and she easily made the freshman basketball squad. However, an unforeseen problem did rear its ugly head after a few weeks of school had passed. Buffy called me at work one day, to tell me that she had gotten dizzy and almost passed-out while walking down a crowded hall. This was what I was afraid of all along the time about my daughter taking these powerful diet pills. The big, negative thing about these heavy uppers, was that the patient (like Buffy or me) often didn't feel like eating anything at all, and then before you know it, you have become weak and unable to function in your daily life.

We gradually had to wean Buffy off the diet pills for her health's sake. She was now getting heavy doses of exercise every day in her training workouts, and that helped immensely. She had lost about 35 pounds total and was easily maintaining her weight-loss. She was in no stretch of the imagination a perfect body size, but she was big-framed and could carry some extra weight well. She no longer struggled getting up and down the basketball court like before. Her 9th and 10th grade sports years were a great success, largely due to her triumphant weight-loss.

On down the road during her later high school years, she had put some of the unwanted pounds back. That sounds an awful lot like her mother (me). One particularly memorable "fat" tale that we often lovingly relay amongst our friends and family is "Buffy's famous dead horse story".

She had gone away for the weekend with one of her girlfriends. This teenager's family had a farm in East Texas, so Buffy was eager to see all the farm animals and she was especially excited to ride one of their many horses.

Buffy didn't really have much experience in horseback riding, but she was up for the invitation that day anyway. The girls rode off slowly across the pastureland. They had been gone for about an hour before her parents spotted the girls heading back to the ranch house. It was a bright, sunny, and warm day there in that part of Texas, and both the girls and the horses were working up a good sweat. Suddenly, Buffy's horse collapsed and fell over on his side, trapping one of her legs underneath the huge animal. Her parents took off running toward them screaming. The horse was so still that they feared he had suffered a heart attack and died right there on the spot. The dad was mainly worried about getting the expensive saddle off the horse's back, the mother was trying her best to revive the poor animal, while Buffy's leg was being crushed. No one seemed to worry about her in the grand scheme of things that were happening. After a few more minutes, and after the saddle had been removed, the seemingly "dead" horse quickly got to his feet and ran off into the woods behind the house.

Buffy concluded after the ordeal, that the horse must have had a weight limit in-tact, and that she must have exceeded the equine's scales. Thus, the smart stallion had feigned death to get her off his back. From then on, Buffy proclaimed that if she ever decided to ride a horse again, that it would have to be the Anheiser Busch variety, the humungous Clydesdale model, like seen in the beer commercials on television.

CHAPTER 13

Time to Take a Chance

Long about the time Amber was about two years old (1981), I had really let my weight problem get totally out of hand. I had gained about 75 pounds when I was pregnant with Amber, and I don't think I lost an ounce after her delivery. In 1981 I began hearing about a new weight-loss phenomenon called gastro-plasty, or stomach-stapling. I made myself an appointment with a well-known Dallas gastro specialist and we entered the doctor's waiting room, cram-packed with anxious yet hopeful fatties.

After a while, Don and I were ushered into the consultation room. This specialist described that the condition I found myself in was clinically labeled "morbid obesity". This kind of scared me, so I asked him to further enlighten me about what that term really meant.

MORBID OBESITY is defined as "a medical condition in which excess body fat has accumulated to the extent that it may have a negative effect on health, leading to reduced life expectancy and/or increased health problems". This definition is from "Wikipedia".

The doctor went on to explain the advantages and disadvantages of this weight-loss method. He outlined the steps that would be used in this new innovative procedure, clinically called the gastro-bypass. He went over the risks involved, and he also warned that many couples end up in a divorce because of the success of the overweight partner and his/her drastic results.

I kind of laughed to myself over that little tidbit. I could not fathom Don and me splitting-up over me losing weight, of all things. The doctor said that he would check with our insurance companies and see if I might be a successful candidate. Also, he wanted us both to go home and think about everything we had discussed in our consultation, including even the remote possibility of our marriage ending in a divorce.

A few short weeks later, I had passed all the required medical tests and I had been approved for the surgery. I checked into one of Dallas' best and largest hospitals for my procedure. I was totally overwhelmed when I saw the wing of the hospital where a lot of guinea pigs like me were all in line for this "miracle" weight-loss surgery. In fact, I learned that some of the surgery candidates were so large that they had to be weighed on grain elevator (industrial-type) scales. Also, I had noticed some extra-large hospital beds, and these were used for the extremely obese patients, the kind that weighed-in at extreme amounts like 500, 600, or even 700 pounds before surgery.

The clear majority of the surgery and procedures were outlined for me prior to being admitted to the hospital, but some rather startling facts were not mentioned at all. I made it through the basic gastro-plasty surgery fine, but I was shocked to wake-up in recovery and find that my main I.V. was attached to me through a jugular vein in my neck. I don't know about you, but just thinking about that connection gives me the willies. If that I.V. was to break loose, I could probably bleed to death almost instantaneously.

In addition, when I had been wheeled back to my regular room, I felt like I had been run over by an eighteen-wheeler. I was still nauseous and sick to death at my stomach from the overload of anesthesia. Once the wave of that illness was over, I began to feel some better. The next trials that I had to endure were the every-four-hour shots in the stomach area. These were to make sure that I did not develop any blood clots, particularly in my legs while my body was at rest. The main and on-going trouble seemed to be the necessity of me being turned over to make sure that I could assume different positions in the bed, especially to help with circulation. I was so huge and so sore now that I could scarcely move, even with the help of the nurses and other physical therapy aides.

I did alright the first few days in the hospital, but the nights were very hard for me. I couldn't really get comfortable to sleep, so I was completely worn-out and in such dire need of some rest.

I also had difficulty getting in and out of bed to complete the daily walking up and down the halls, per doctor orders. I had been cut from under my bust line, all the way down to my navel. It was not an easy thing for a 288-pound woman to maneuver with a ton of her muscles cut in-two. It was a good thing that I was only twenty-five years old at the time. An added plus was that I was still teaching baton twirling lessons, so that had somewhat kept me in shape, despite the heavy, excessive weight that I had been carrying around for years.

The doctor finally ordered a liquid diet for me and I seemed to do ok with the broths, gelatins, and sugar-free ice pops. I seemed to be progressing as well as could be expected.

After six full days in the hospital, the doctor said that I could go home on the seven day --- IF --- I could tolerate a full regular-diet meal for dinner that evening. I was so excited to get to have real solid food, but I was also afraid to try-out my new tiny stomach. So far, I had only sampled easy, liquid foods and I had done great on those.

The time had come for the real test to take place. I couldn't imagine what "good" food might be coming my way that evening – perhaps steak, chicken, some kind of meat casserole, etc.? But, no. You wouldn't believe what they tried-out my new stomach with. It was a corned beef sandwich, of all things!

Definition from Wikipedia, the free encyclopedia......

"Corned beef is a salt-cured beef product. The term comes from the treatment of the meat with large grained rock salt, also called "corns" of salt."

Just so you understand, corned beef is a tough, stringy kind of meat to digest, even on a regular stomach. I took very small bites as directed, and downed about half of the sandwich over a period of about thirty to forty-five minutes. I thought I had done an admirable job in eating my first solid food, but such was not the case a few hours later.

Around eleven o'clock that same evening, I began to throw-up and I didn't stop until I had upchucked thirteen different times during the night. If you can only imagine how much pain I was in while my body heaved and rejected my first real meal after surgery. I was in complete agony, trying to hold a pillow over my stitched-up mid-section while completing the task of vomiting over several hours. I can tell you that I was starting to rethink my decision for this major surgery. And it was one heck of a night for me to endure.

At least prior to surgery, I was very overweight but in pretty good general health. Now I didn't know what I had done to myself and wondered how I could un-fix it!!! By the next morning I was feeling better, but completely afraid to try and eat solid foods now. The doctor sent me on home, but I still can't get over why the hospital dietician would have approved such a harsh and hard-to-digest type of food like corned beef. Or, maybe my doctor didn't realize what the nutritionist had on the menu for that night. Either way, I was a basket case on my way home.

The one, good positive thing that I would hold onto was the fact that the hospital had weighed me before my departure, and I was already down thirteen pounds in one week's time. I was eager to see what my future might hold for me in the days and weeks ahead.

My first important task to be completed each morning was my trip to my newly acquired scales. I would confidently step up on my all-time nemesis, and then face the numbers bravely every day. It was no longer a hurtful experience, but rather a welcomed sight when I would have usually lost a pound or two every single day. It seemed to be the easier thing in the world. Why hadn't someone come up with this quick-fix years ago?

Over the course of the next few weeks, I was weak and tired, but that was to be expected since I could hardly eat the smallest of small amounts of food. I was literally living on about a handful of food a day. I could not believe that I could possibly be full, but I was. My entire meal now was about the size of one serving of a vegetable, back in my pre-surgery days.

Pounds seemed to be dropping off very easily, but then I ran into a sort of brick wall. One morning I woke up feeling poorly, and I continued to throw up for most of the day. Again, I panicked and started wondering why I had allowed the doctor to do this to me. All sorts of diseases were dancing around in my head, so I phoned the weight-loss doctor and set up an appointment for the following day.

I entered the doctor's office very sick and anxious to find out what terrible thing was happening to my new body. Low and behold, it turned out to be a simple stomach virus, nothing major at all. In fact, I told the doctor how nervous I was about not being able to eat and how I feared getting dehydrated. He chuckled and simply said, "Patty, you have so much fat stored-up in your body that you could probably go without eating for three months and you'd be just fine". (Jeez...... Here we go with the "fat jokes", even after the weight loss surgery! That's all I needed – was a comedic doctor.)

I guess he had proven his point to me, but it hurt my "fat girl" feelings all the same. The pounds were melting away, but my sensitivity was still there lurking around in full force.

A few months of learning to eat a new way, and I had started an unhealthy pattern of getting rid of even more unwanted pounds. I had become accustomed to the bad feeling I would get in my small stomach when I had eaten something that didn't agree with my system. I would instantly start to feel my mouth watering and I would quickly find the nearest bathroom so I could gag myself and then throw-up to get rid of the disagreeable food item.

I didn't think about it much when this first started happening, but after a time I began to wonder about me becoming bulimic. That is someone that overeats and then practices self-induced vomiting, purging, or fasting. I had started doing this very thing more often as I tried to adapt to my new way of eating and keeping my food down.

I knew that I certainly wasn't ultra-thin like singer Karen Carpenter, who passed away in 1983 from the terrible disease of bulimia. But still I thought to myself, "Wouldn't that be an odd coincidence if I died from not eating enough?"

My stomach finally settled down after a few more months, and I didn't encounter much of the throwing-up problem much at all. Over the next year I had miraculously dropped right at one hundred pounds. I was so proud of myself and felt totally amazing. I began to realize that my backaches were gone, as well as the problems with my feet. It still took size 16 or 18 clothing to fit me, but that was shades better than having to shop at the fat lady stores in the past.

Call me paranoid, but I began to feel differently about myself and my appearance. And this wasn't always a good thing. In fact, some of what the weight-loss doctor had mentioned in mine and Don's first consultation, the part about this surgery sometimes causing a divorce, was already coming into play in my new life.

Suddenly, men began to notice me. Some would comment about how good I looked, and some even out-and-out flirted with me. I was getting all this new attention that I hadn't had since my early days of high school. I even had some men in my office ask me to lunch some days. I particularly didn't like the ones that had previously treated me like I was so fat that I part of the wall. I would think...... "So, now that I've lost weight, you are acknowledging me, huh??? No way would I ever give you the time of day. If you can only accept me now that I've lost weight, then I have no time for you --- the same way that you had no time for me previously when I was one of those detestable fat people".

During the mid-eighties the country went through a time of "Urban Cowboy" frenzy, based on the John Travolta and Debra Winger movie by the same name. It was like everybody was suddenly into boot-scootin', so one of my male co-workers invited me to come and see him and his partner dance in a country and western competition in a well-known Dallas club. I decided to check them out one night, and the result was me getting him signed-up to teach dance lessons to a group of my friends that all lived in my own home town.

We had so much fun once a week with this guy instructor. We would teach us a new country and western dance each week, and then we'd spend the remainder of our lesson time practicing what we had learned. I even got my mother to sign-up for the lessons. She and my father had been jitterbug champions back in the early fifties, but now that she was much older, I didn't know how she might fare.

Well, as it turned out, my mother was the hit of the class each week. She would sometimes trip and fall during the lessons, and we'd all have to stop and take time-out to laugh with her. One night she got so tickled at a new step that she couldn't seem to catch, that she started laughing so hard that she wet her pants. And then all the rest of us got tickled, so more laughing than dancing took place that week. In fact, the instructor told me privately that he couldn't wait to see my mother each week at the lessons, as we never knew what she might do next to keep us in stitches!

One of my best friends Lena and I came up with a new dance called the "Hun and Bun Shuffle". We actually debutted it at a local dance hall named Bear Creek Crossing. She was "Hun", and , of course, I was "Bun". Oh what fun times we had dancing!

After the dance lessons started to fizzle-out, the instructor and I seemed to continue our friendship outside of the office – so much so that he asked me to go to a music concert in Dallas. He knew I was married and I thought he might be gay, but I went on with him anyway. There is no way that I would ever have gotten Don Hullett to go with me to a Diana Ross concert, so I went on with my man friend. I thought this would be a harmless night out away from my family.

Before the concert was over, he had talked me into leaving the arena and going with him to a dance place. He grabbed my hand, led me through the crowd, and all I could think about was if someone ever saw me holding hands with another man, I would die. I had to keep in mind that I was married to a man at home who would be fuming if he knew where I was and what I was doing.

We got to the club and I danced with him for a few songs. It was so much fun because he was such a terrific partner. However, I looked around but hadn't noticed so many men in the building. Then, just as I had suspected, he left me on the sidelines and went to dance with a "man". I guess I truly deserved this insult. Here I was, a married woman, running around with another man, and I get slapped in the face with the fact that he has brought me to a gay dance hall. I couldn't wait to drop him off at his house and then_to get myself on home. I had come to the stark realization that he had used me as a front for his being gay, especially at work, to deflect the fact that he was different. And stupid me, I took it all in -- hook, line and sinker. Driving myself the long way home gave me some much-needed time to think about how I let myself get roped-into a situation like this.

Maybe the doctor had been right. Sometimes married couples do get divorced after one partner loses a tremendous amount of weight. But hopefully, this was my wake-up call. I promised myself that I would get my head screwed-on straight and perhaps avoid a possible divorce situation after all. What in the world was I thinking, running around with another man when I was married?

Now that men were starting to notice me, Don became excessively jealous and accusing. It seemed like we were always arguing about something. And it seemed that I was almost always up and ready for a good fight, too. Our once air-tight, forever marriage was quickly deflating in a big way.

And it certainly didn't help that my husband was lazy and didn't like to go to work every day. He kept changing jobs like someone changes clothes. It was killing us financially because he would bounce from job to job, with lots of downtime and no pay checks in-between. After a few weeks or a couple of months of not working, he would then start another new endeavor.

About that time, I added another evening job to my occupational resume. In addition to my teaching baton lessons a couple of weeknights, I had started attending several home decorating parties endorsed by a company called *"Home Interiors and Gifts, Inc."*. I was spending so much money on furnishing our home that I determined that I might as well become a sales consultant so I would get some of their major discounts. In other words, I was working three jobs, while my husband couldn't seem to hold down one.

This Christian-based direct sales company was started by a single mom by the name of Mary C. Crowley in Dallas in 1957. The mostly-women sales representatives sold home decorating accessories by way of home parties. Many of the items that I offered at my shows featured plaques with Bible verses on them and other Christian home décor pieces. To me, my newest job just didn't seem to fit me, especially when I hadn't gone to church in years.

After a while, I concluded that I was nothing more than a hypocrite peddling my wares based on the principles of my godly company. It made me feel disgusted with myself, knowing that I hadn't set foot in a church building since I was a teenager. And lately I certainly had done plenty of other things that made me a prime candidate for a large portion of much-needed repentance from my Lord.

The added friction that Don and I were undergoing wasn't helping the situation either. I cried myself to sleep many a night, wondering if I should divorce him or try to hang on and somehow make our marriage work. One thing was certain. I wanted to make a change, because I didn't want my two daughters to have quarreling parents and a bad family life like I often experienced growing up.

I had become completely fed-up with our constant financial struggles because Don didn't want to pull his weight and work like a regular husband trying to take care of his family. I felt so bitter and broken because I was the only one bearing the burdens of our flailing marriage. I thought long and hard, and finally realized there was only one place I could go to in this instance....back to church to try and repair my relationship with Jesus Christ. I knew in my heart that He was the only one that could possibly restore the brokenness of our marriage.

From the time I was about 3 years old, my parents wouldn't take me to church, but they would drop me off at a local Sunday School class. I never understood why my parents didn't go with me, but in looking back, I know I was blessed to get that opportunity, as some children never had that chance.

I simply loved going to church, and I especially lived for Vacation Bible School classes in the summer. It was during my pre-teen years I took an even bigger step of faith by staying for the traditional service most every Sunday.

One day I remember sitting all by myself in that big church building and I began to cry when I realized that I was a sinner and I needed God in my life. That very day I walked down that long, lonely aisle of the sanctuary and made the smartest decision of my life. I accepted Christ as my Savior and was baptized that evening. I even talked my mother and daddy into coming to see me that special night.

But at my age, it was hard to maintain a constant walk of faith in my daily life when I wasn't being raised in a Christian family setting. As a new believer, I felt I was a stronger person on the inside, but I was very timid about sharing my new way of life with others. With not much support from my family, I prayed every night, but I wasn't living my life out-loud as a Christ-follower. Instead, I was somewhat a "closet" Christian.

So, I had become a Christ-follower when I was eleven years old, but when I got on up into high school I didn't think it was so cool being a "goody two-shoes". Or, at least that was the excuse I kept telling myself as to why I quit going to church on Sundays. Perhaps it could have been because I knew I was a part of things that I knew were not right in the sight of Lord.

As more and more trouble filled my adult life, I began to realize how skewed my way of thinking had become. I had slowly let the devil back into my life. But during my early teen years, I guess I was too worried about my reputation and what my friends might think. I just couldn't see myself being one of those Bible-thumping Jesus freaks when I was having the time of my life in high school.

But now, when I found myself sinking in the sea of married life, I made a covenant with God that I would start attending church regularly. If not only for my marital issues with my husband, then also to "fix" my damaged relationship with God.

Ready to start over again, I randomly selected a nearby Baptist church one Sunday morning, especially since I had been raised in that particular denomination. I took my two young daughters with me to try one final thing to hold onto my marriage. Call it luck or name it my divine destiny, but I felt secure and at home amid this wonderful, accepting congregation. I also loved the pastor, especially since he quoted his own homemade poetry that he recited throughout his message. Poetry had always held a special place in my heart. I found that this church and this preacher were an excellent fit for what I needed in my life at that time.

I asked Don to attend church with me, but he was having none of my suggestion. Therefore, I kept going week after week without him. I had started to development some friends there and I even joined the Sunday School class for my age group. After a couple of months had passed I found that Don started asking me questions about my experiences at the church services each week. I told him that it was fun, uplifting, and educational – that he ought to just give it a try some Sunday.

Before I realized it, I was a regular attender, I had made some friends, and I felt better that I'd felt in a long, long time. My husband didn't have much of a church background at all while he was growing up, but he showed some interest and began to ask me about my church. Things like...... "What do you do every week? What is the pastor like? Are the people friendly?"

It wasn't too long until Don decided to give the "church thing" a try himself. One Sunday was all it took. Don liked the fellowship and the teaching he was getting, so he began attending with me every week. Not only did it stop most of our marital bickering, but it seemed to mend a lot of the hurts we had been inflicting on each other. The entire family was now going to church every Sunday, and we all liked it.

In October of 1981, Don was employed by a major airline at that time, but he had seriously injured his back while loading and unloading provisions into the galleys of the planes. In fact, he was about to undergo a second back surgery within a two-year time span. This procedure was to repair a ruptured disc, and Don was very worried about his chances of a full recovery and his ability to return to his old job at the airport.

I was trying to work every hour I could, leading up until the time of his operation. I knew he would be off work and out of commission for a few months, so I was hoping to work as many hours as possible. From his hospital room he called me one morning at work. He simply wanted to know if I could ask our new pastor if he would be willing to come by and visit him before his surgery the following morning. I told him that I would call the church and ask.

After a couple of hours passed I received yet another phone call from Don, and he was ecstatic. He explained to me that the preacher had visited him and he had accepted Christ as his Savior right then and there from his hospital bed. He had committed to being baptized in a few weeks after his back had healed.

I was overjoyed at Don's decision, and I thought this huge important step in his life might just save our marriage. On a side note, I later wrote a personal letter to Mary C. Crowley and told her what a blessed Christmas we were enjoying that year after my reconnecting to a church and following the baptism of my new-born, Christian husband. God had used my part-time job at *"Home Interiors"* to reach both of us, and He had intervened in His perfect timing! With His help, we had a new hope for our future together.

What a changed man Don became over the next couple of years! He had been transformed into a responsible husband, father and provider. No more being lazy and not protecting his family as the head of the household. Our marriage was back on track and we became true Christ-followers in every sense of the word. You see....God is still in the business of performing miracles – in circumstances and in people!

CHAPTER 14

The Brazilian Way to Host
an Exchange Student

If the Hullett family didn't have enough drama and action going on already, Don decided that we needed to test the waters for a foreign exchange student to host. The year was 1983, and we were heavily involved in our church, our jobs, and we also coached two soccer teams. Don oversaw Buffy's age group (Girls Under 12), and I was enjoying Amber's mixed boy and girl team ("Under 6").

Over my strong objections, Don pressed on by ordering a stack of student profiles of foreign teenagers seeking temporary housing in America. The program we became a part of, was for students either wanting a six-month or full year stint of living and experiencing high school life in the good ole U.S.A.

As a family, we would sit down in the evenings and peruse each student packet – looking at each candidate's personality, hobbies/interests, church background, and profile photos. We unanimously chose a beautiful seventeen-year old girl named Sandra. This Brazilian young lady seemed to be a good fit for our family.

Next, Don talked to our American counselor and placement advisor. She came to our home and interviewed the four of us. A few days later we were "approved" to be an acceptable host home for student placement.

In turn, Sandra then "approved" our request to host her, and we immediately set about getting our home ready to receive a new member into our household for a period of one full school semester (or approximately a stay of six months in the U.S.). In January of 1984, we counted-down the days until we finally headed to the Dallas / Fort Worth International Airport to pick-up our long-awaited exchange student from the South American country of Brazil.

Armed with "welcome" posters and banners, the kids were eager to meet their new addition to our family. Once we saw her appear from the jetway, we knew it was love at first sight. This beyond-gorgeous girl had a shining smile that lit-up the entire airport.

We all greeted her and gave her hugs, but we instantaneously came across one small problem with our perfect "Sandy". It seemed that she had forgotten to tell us one tiny thing. She couldn't really speak English, as her profile incorrectly stated.

On the long, uncomfortable ride home, we ascertained that she only knew and understood three English words ---- YES, NO, and BEAUTIFUL. That was the extent of her understanding our native language. This was going to be quite an interesting school semester ahead of us all.

After the first few days in our country, we drove through the main streets of downtown Dallas and then further to far North Dallas for shopping at a new, exclusive new mall. We wanted to impress her, so we took her to the finest mall in the DFW area at that time.

Sandy wanted to purchase a few more outfits prior to starting at her new high school. While she was busy trying on clothes, we sat outside of the dressing room, just waiting for her to model her selections. She would ask for our opinion, and then she would quickly return to the fitting area.

When it was time leave, she realized that someone had taken her purse off the hook in her dressing room stall. She broke down and started to cry. And it was not just a little crying. It was a lot of tears. In fact, she was so hard to console that we thought she might be ready to pack-up and go back home to Brazil.

I tried to assure her that I had shopped in Dallas my entire life and had never had anything stolen from me. I felt so terrible for her. What a bad first impression she must have gotten from our first failed shopping excursion in Dallas, Texas.

After we got to our car and got Sandy settled down, we, at last, fully comprehended her biggest fear. It was not the fact that she had lost quite a bit of American cash (her daddy's money), plus some international traveler cheques. In actuality, she was forlorn over the fact that her "Portuguese to English" translation book had been in her purse! She realized that she would no longer have a way to communicate in English at her new school.

The problem was solved in one breakneck stop at a *"Half Price Book Store"*. Thankfully, we found Sandy's new favorite and most-treasured little book. The day was saved!

With the new school semester upon us, our new daughter wanted to show us her swimming suits, as she wanted to try-out for her high school's swim team. She admitted that she enjoyed competing in meets back in her home town of Recife, but she confirmed that her parents had never come to see her swim – in person. Not one time had they been there to support her in her sport.

First, Sandy came prancing out of the bathroom in a one-piece "thong" swimsuit. Our eyes almost popped-out when she did a model turn to reveal the rear view of her classic Brazilian swim attire. We had to promptly explain to her, that despite her looking perfect with her perfect figure, she must choose another suit for school swimming try-outs. We did our best con convince her to make a more modest selection of suits.

Sandy finally understood. She exclaimed, with the assistance of her "Portuguese to English" book, "I have one more suit to show you."

Sure enough, it was a one-piece, plain but very classy suit, that covered-up her rear end in a tasteful way. Thank goodness, another dilemma had been solved.

When the first day of class rolled around, Sandy looked beautiful as we led her into a humungous, bustling high school that was so large that it more aptly looked like a college campus. I was so afraid of unleashing our sweet Sandy into an unsuspecting sea of high school boys that turned and stared as she walked down the halls of her new school. I took in a big, nervous breath, as we headed toward the registration office to enroll our exchange student.

After checking her in, we walked her to her first class with the help of an office aide. The class had already begun, but the teacher politely stopped her lesson and introduced Sandy to the group. I could see and feel her apprehension at this point, but the teacher broke the silence by letting everyone know that Sandy had limited English skills. Straightaway, several young guys approached Don and me, and asked if we could communicate with Sandy and to tell her that they thought she was "beautiful".

Sandy then batted her exquisite eyelashes and stunned the entire classroom with her gorgeous smile. And now that she was feeling more comfortable, we left her to fend for herself. The other students seem to be extending the hand of friendship to her, and especially the guys with their tongues hanging-out because of her special beauty.

One afternoon she came home from school, almost in tears. Someone had broken into her swim locker and taken her hair dryer, shampoo, and other supplies. Now, we even felt worse for the second bad impression that our country must have made on Sandy. Within a month's time in the U.S., she had been the unlucky recipient of two different theft situations. First, a crook had stolen her purse at an upscale mall, and now, she had been ripped-off by a student thief taking her swim accessories at her high school locker room. I felt so badly because of the unfortunate circumstances that she had experienced in our safe and welcoming country.

One thing was certain. Sandy missed her Brazilian staple of her beloved black beans, so we appeased her by buying her several cans from our local supermarket. However, it didn't take but a few more weeks until she had fallen in love with our high-calorie, and very appealing fast foods. Very quickly her favorite treats became McDonald's pancakes, Hershey chocolate bars, and all types of Mexican food.

Our exchange student had entered our country at the ideal weight of around 115 pounds. She was such a beauty and so perfectly proportioned that our family felt she could have easily been named "Miss Brazil". But it didn't take the overweight Hullett family long to corrupt this health-conscientious young lady to leave her light-eating ways behind. We had promptly turned her in to a fast food junky!

Sandy began to slowly speak and understand our English language much better, yet she never left our house without her "Portuguese to English" book. She and her helpful book were inseparable.

Sandy began to realize that her clothes were getting tighter and tighter. Almost every Sunday she would announce to us in her very best English diction, "Tomorrow I go on diet." (Sounded a lot like some of my famous last words.) However, "diet Monday" never seemed to come. She simply loved our food, so much so that she couldn't get her weight-gain under control.

In the spring, a few months after her arrival her in America, Sandy's dad, who was a doctor, attended a medical convention in Chicago. He planned a two-day layover in the Dallas area, so he could visit his daughter that he had been missing so very much.

As Luis deplaned, emerged from the jetway, and spotted his Sandy, he instantly noticed the added weight on his daughter's frame. He particularly kidded her by pinching both of her facial cheeks and asking her, "What happened to you, Sandy?"

Unfortunately, it was not entirely her fault. She had been overtaken by the Family Hullett and their terrible eating habits.

It was so much fun having Sandy in our home. She was a constant source of laughter. Because of her challenge in speaking and understanding English, we would purposely put her in *"I Love Lucy"* situations. We love d to play the game of "Pictionary". You can only imagine our comedic value in watching Sandy flip through her translation book at light speed, so she could locate the correct English word for the game. We would laugh at her until we cried. And she was always such a good sport about it.

Sandy worked hard each weekday to be part of her huge school's swim team. When competition time came around, the Hullett clan, who knew nothing about the sport of swimming, turned out in full force, just eagerly wanting to see our athletic Sandy. We came to support her, especially since her Brazilian parents never came to see her in her meets back home.

Her school had a large, winning swim program, so even though we had hoped for the best, Sandy inevitably came in last place in every event at every competition. It didn't really matter to us. We always supported her – win or lose. We cheered her on, no matter the outcome.

Don's dad was the manager of a grocery chain's credit union. He hosted a national credit union convention in Dallas while Sandy was living with us, and he asked our entire family to attend. It was a high-toned affair, and the main course of food was very expensive prime rib. Beside the delicious meat was a dollop of spicy, raw horseradish. Before we could answer Sandy's question of, "What is this?", she had popped the scoop of red-hot goodness into her mouth.

We could almost see the smoke coming out of Sandy's ears. We had tried to describe horseradish to her and how hot it was, but it was much too late! The damage had already been done.

Another time, we had taken Sandy out to eat dinner at a Chinese restaurant. After the excellent Asian meal, Sandy did it again. She popped the unknown fortune cookie into her mouth, then hesitated when she happened upon the paper fortune in her mouth. She exclaimed (again), "What is this?" It was then time to explain the fortune cookie and the paper message inside.

School had let out in May, it was almost summer, and since Sandy only had a few more weeks left in the U.S., we decided to take our two daughters, plus our student, to a special campground in the State of Oklahoma. There were some beautiful falls there, and it emptied into a nice natural pool for the girls to swim in.

Over the six months that Sandy had lived with us, there had been a complete transformation of her exhibition of showing-off her body like she had when she first arrived in our country. She had become so shy to display her body, that we had to force her to take off her swimsuit cover-up and to join our daughters in the warm and inviting water.

A large group of college guys had hit the pool about the same time that Sandy had finally made it into the pool. Don and I could tell that most of these young men had definitely noticed our drop-dead gorgeous Sandy, even with a few extra pounds. We saw them whispering amongst themselves, and then a few minutes later, they began to sing a song to Sandy from the movie, *"Top Gun"* – *"You've Lost that Loving Feeling"* – by the Righteous Brothers.

Sandy got so embarrassed by all the attention that she slipped out of the water and put back on her cover-up and refused to expose herself in the bathing suit the remainder of our camping trip. Boy, had we made her feel self-conscientious, or what?

That evening when we went to bed in our tents, we all went to sleep easily, except for Sandy. She woke us up around midnight, yelling that it was raining outside and that we needed to get our "foots" into the tent.

We tried to assure her that all our "foots" were securely safe inside the tents. She just kept on and on, until we realized that she was talking about our "foods" – not our "foots". Some of our picnic items had been left at the door of our tents. Quickly, we rescued our provisions and thanked Sandy for waking us up and letting us know. She couldn't seem to go to sleep by sleeping on the ground. She asked me, point-blank, "Why you do this? Why do you want to sleep on the hard ground?"

I laughed and then explained that sleeping on the ground and in tents, is what you do when you go on a "camping" trip.

At last, she asked me if I would go with her and sleep in the comfortable car. I agreed, and therefore, she and I slept soundly inside of our automobile. I don't think our little, spoiled rich girl enjoyed her camping experience at all.

After another week or so, it was time to say our goodbyes to our sweet, one-of-a-kind exchange student. We all cried like babies at the airport to see her off. She had genuinely made positive impact on our Hullett family. We would most definitely miss our fun and always exciting girl from Brazil.

And much to her chagrin, Sandy was leaving Texas and heading to her home city in Brazil, approximately twenty pounds heavier in the short span of seven months with our wild and crazy and fat family.

Poor, Sandy…. The first thing her mother did was put her daughter back on a very strict diet to get rid of those unwanted pounds!

We must say that after hosting exchange students from around the world (Australia, France, The Czech Republic, Japan), our favorite folks on the planet are the Brazilians. A total of four students came from our South America's jewel – Brazil. Besides Sandy, we hosted two sisters that we loved immensely – Patricia and Bella, and then a rather strange boy named Luciano. We deeply loved these sweet teenagers because they were fun-loving, laid-back, and very adaptable to our different American ways. It was a blast getting to know the country of Brazil by hosting four of their wonderful students.

CHAPTER 15

Another Star's Time to Shine

About the time that Buffy turned ten, her little sister Amber started her career in sports as well. Unlike Buffy, known for her brawn, Amber was little and wiry. I first coached a mixed boy/girl soccer team for Amber in the "Under 6" age division in our city. Unfortunately, we were the only "mixed" team. All the other competing teams consisted of boys exclusively. I felt a little handicapped with about the same number of girls and boys on my team. But by the same token, I felt blessed to have some truly athletic little ladies.

We had won most of our games that first season, but had lost a close one to a male-dominated team coached by an A-typical chauvinistic man that totally looked down at my team being led by a woman. Then it came time for a play-off for first place in the "Under 6" division. The arrogant boys' coach taunted Amber by asking her, "Are you still going to speak to me after we get through beating you, Amber?" I was standing there with my mouth opened and couldn't believe he would try to intimidate a four-year old girl.

I don't remember the exact score, but what I do know is that we beat his "rough and tough" all boys' team. And the contest wasn't even close. Our girl/boy team took first place in our inaugural season in the "Under 6" boys' age group. Way to go, Under 6 Duncanville "All-Stars".

After a couple of more seasons of soccer, Amber became so good in the field that a boys' team picked her up for defensive help. She became a very successful sweeper that played in front of the defensive fullbacks. A lot of games the three fullbacks didn't get much action, because our girl was busy keeping the other team's offense back-tracking. We had nicknamed our soccer girl "Ambo" (instead of "Amber"), but she played so physical during the games that her teammates changed her name into "Rambo" (from the Sylvester Stallone movie).

From there, Amber also started playing some softball in the summers, but she would get so frustrated playing on girls' teams. She got along well with the tomboy girls that gave 100 per cent of their effort. But she couldn't stomach the little sissy girls that would scream and then drop the easy popped-fly during a softball game. She just didn't understand why most of the other girls didn't care as much and didn't give as much effort as she did.

I recall one year in the summer softball league, they were short on coaches, so I volunteered to oversee a team in Amber's age division. The city held a play day try-out in front of the proposed coaches. Each girl was to hit, throw, and catch to show-off their skills, or lack thereof. At the end of the day, each coach was to select fourteen or fifteen players for his/her own team.

I had chosen one young lady that seemed to be quite athletic and I thought she might fit well on Amber's team. The next day after try-outs, and before I had even contacted my selected girls, this certain girl's mother phoned to ask me some questions. The mom told me that another coach had relayed the information that her daughter was chosen to be on my team. I confirmed that "yes", I had picked her daughter.

So, she went on to ask me the main focal point of her phone call. She bluntly asked me what I looked like. At first, I didn't comprehend what she was getting at during our conversation.

I answered her by saying that "I was wearing a bright pink shirt during the try-outs".

But she continued with her same line of questioning by asking one final defining conundrum....... "Are you a large or small woman?"

I was somewhat taken back by her question, but not to disillusion her at all, I promptly responded, "I am the large woman that was wearing pink. So, what about it?"

She very boldly then told me that her daughter did not want to play for my team, but what she was implying was that she didn't think I knew anything about softball based on my size and unathletic appearance.

That turned-out to be perfectly fine with we, as my team trampled her little darling's squad every time we played them that summer. Karma can sometimes come back to bite you in the rear end, so be careful what you wish for!

Amber continued to be successful in most of her sports attempts; however, she would get so frustrated when her soccer and softball girlfriends chose to back-off from any physical contact on the sports fields. Most of the females just didn't play with the same amount of heart and enthusiasm that she did.

Her constant intrepid thirst to be a part of a winning team caused her to change her total sports focus at the age of ten. She had suddenly become interested in playing tennis in a local summer instructional league. At the end of the summer, when the group lessons were concluding, they played a one-day beginners' tournament. Don and I both took off work to come and see our daughter play, and she did not disappoint. In fact, Amber won the 1st place trophy in her age group.

She decided to continue-on in tennis, saying that it was a great "individual" sport, one that she could win or lose at, and she didn't have to depend on anyone else. Tennis results would totally be up to her, and no one else. She also liked the fact that Don and I knew absolutely nothing about tennis, so it was a bonus to her that we would not be able to coach her. She had created her very own, new sport to excel in.

The following summer and thereafter, Amber looked forward to the group tennis lessons. She and her closest competitor both completed the summer classes together for several years in a row. In fact, Amber would take first one year, and then it seemed like the next year the other young lady would capture first, with Amber coming in second. They both loved the rivalry and good, honest competition that they enjoyed playing against each other for the top spot of the summer session.

After a couple of summers of completing the summer camps, Amber's instructor even encouraged her further by urging her to try her hand at outside "United States Tennis Association" ("U.S.T.A.") competitive tennis tournaments. As I mentioned previously, my husband and I were very sports-minded, but tennis was a thing that neither of us knew much about at all. We did take the advice of the summer coach, so at age eleven we entered Amber in her first "outside" tennis event in a city about an hour and a half away from Dallas.

By the time Amber had started tennis the "fat bug" had bitten her, too. Our next stepping stone in her tennis career became the hard challenge of finding an outfit that would fit her little chubby frame for her first tournament. She was just about as wide as she was tall at this stage in her life. Most of the ready-made Adidas, Reebok, and Nike shirts and skirts were made for the typical cookie-cutter size young girl. But because of Amber's larger-sized body, we had to spend quite a lot of money to find a women's size Reebok matching tennis shirt and skirt that would fit her. In fact, the skirt was a little too long, but it would have to do based on the limited selection and our budget. Amber somehow always exuded confidence, even in the middle of her fat-related adversity. She simply thought that she was looking so cool that someone might suspect her of being one of the U.S.T.A. tour players! That is just how confident she looked in her new outfit, and she was so proud to wear it at her very first meet.

Don and I sat up high in the roost seating, looking down on the multi-courts below. When it was finally time for Amber to compete in her first match, all of us were nervous with excitement. The play began and both of us became acutely aware of the fact that her competitor was beginning to make bad calls on the court. If Amber hit a winning shot, the girl would call the ball "out". If the girl's ball was very distinctly out-of-bounds, she would argue with Amber and say that her ball was "in". This happened a couple of times at first, so Amber seemed to just blow it off. I was told that these official U.S.T.A. tournaments didn't feature court monitors to assist the young players with the calls in each point played. The situation was based on an "honor" system. It was just up to each player to be truthful in any close calls during the match.

Amber finally got so discussed with the cheating of this little girl that she started looking up at us in the stands. She had no idea what to do to combat the girl's dishonesty. She would give us a shrug of her shoulders to indicate, "What should I do? This girl is cheating me on a lot of the calls." We could tell that she was appalled by the audacity of this young lady to blatantly make horrible calls in front of everyone sitting in the stands as witnesses.

About this time, a very prissy and well-dressed lady headed in my direction. She announced that she was the mother of my daughter's current competitor. She started ranting and raving about us trying to coach our daughter from the stands, and that it was not allowed by U.S.T.A. rules. I apologized and told her that this was our first outside tournament, and that we were just beginning to learn all the tennis rules. The rude lady then pointedly told us that we needed to learn some tennis etiquette, as she turned on her heels and marched back to her seat. That made me fighting mad, especially since most everybody in the stands knew that her daughter was trying her best to cheat my Amber out of winning the match. But, not to make a scene, I just held my tongue and let the arrogant lady walk away.

After a while in the competition Amber was so much better of a player, that even with all the cheating, the gal couldn't stay on the court with Amber. My daughter had won her first outside match, despite the dishonesty of the other competitor. A few minutes later both girls had made their way back up into the stands. Amber was standing within earshot of me when the same lady came back to bless me out again. In front of a lot of my friends (and where Amber also heard) she repeated that Don and I needed to learn some tennis etiquette, and then she proceeded to announce out loud that, "Your daughter may have won the tennis match, but she is still a fat slob". I almost fainted at her harsh words, but I quickly gathered myself and responded, "Well, my daughter may be overweight, but she just beat your little skinny kid, so what's her excuse?"

Most of the other tennis mothers that had heard the outrageous statement made by the bad-loser mother, told me that I should have punched her right, smack in her face. Thankfully, I think my comment got my message across anyway.

So very much like what her obese mother (me) had endured before her (Amber), I pulled my daughter aside and advised her that if she really wanted to press on in the sport of tennis, she would have to grow some thick, tough skin. That meant her not letting other people's comments upset her. I advised her that she would probably have to be twice as good as the next player, just to prove to the others that she deserved to win as an overweight young girl. I had plenty of examples in my life that I could share with her to make her know how the world works through the eyes of a fat kid.

If you really knew Amber as a little girl, then it was a known fact that she had always envisioned herself as a cheerleader. A couple of years later she decided that she wanted to try out for cheerleader for her junior high school. I was well-aware that she could successfully complete all the required jumps and even the splits as part of the audition. Wanting to be completely honest with her, I reminded her how difficult it might be in trying out in front of prejudiced judges. Also, my thinking was that cheerleader moms might prove to be some of the worst examples of "stage mothers" ever. I talked to her about all the possible obstacles, but she assured me that she was tough enough to handle it. After all, she was almost 13 years old. She assured me that she had it all under control.

All the wanna-be cheerleaders were taught the selected cheers and jumps for two weeks prior to the actual try-out date. Amber was extremely happy and proud when she came home from try-outs and announced that the cheerleader sponsor (a very nice and supportive school teacher) called her name out as the cheerleader "mascot". That meant that she would do everything that the other cheerleaders did, but she would sometimes have to wear a hawk's head, the mascot of their junior high. It would be up to us to design and come-up with the hawk's head that she would wear ---- but other than that, she would go to cheerleader camp, she would learn the same cheers and dance routine, and she would participate just like the other cheerleaders.

After a couple of weeks into the required practices, I began to hear some negative comments coming from some of the girls, and sometimes repeated words from some of the cheerleader moms. I realized then that this was going to be a hard year for Amber to make it as the school mascot. I was beginning to understand now why some of the little prissy cheerleaders said unkind things to Amber, especially after being around some of the actual mothers. I was starting to see first-hand exactly why the kids acted so rudely. They were being trained by their rude and uncaring mothers. The kids were simply repeating what they heard and learned from their moms at home.

The possible nail in the cheerleader coffin for Amber was the fact that the nice and inclusive school sponsor had decided to move away to another city during the summer. The newly-appointed sponsor was very vocal about the fact that Amber was NOT a real cheerleader. That the way she saw things, Amber must have on the hawk's head all the time. After going to the summer camp and learning all the yells and the dance routine, she was not going to be allowed to join in the real duties of a regular cheerleader. Instead, she was to keep herself as a background person, and she could only encourage others to join the cheerleaders. She was not to do much but stand on the sidelines during the games.

Amber make it through the summer camp experience ok, and it wasn't soon thereafter until school started and the football games began. One evening after one of the team's first games, she came up to me and she was balling her eyes out. I asked her what the problem was, and she told me that the sponsor had gotten on to her for taking her hawk's head off during the game. It was still a very hot evening in Texas for a football game in September, but the lady made it very clear that even though she might get hot, that she must leave on the hawk head at all times. Amber took that to mean that she must have thought that she was so ugly, that she must keep the mascot head on, no matter what. I tried to explain that the woman probably didn't mean the hawk's head comment that way, but Amber wasn't buying it. She felt like the lady thought she was ugly, so she must hide underneath the head. That was "strike one" for the cheerleader project.

The next problem was that we would sit in the football stands in front of the cheerleaders and mascot to help support them in their cheers. It got to where our family would hear some of the junior high kids making fun of Amber for being overweight. One night, Buffy had heard a pretty large boy call her sister "Fatso", and that was all it took. I had no idea where Buffy was going, but she disappeared. A few minutes later she came back to her seat in the stands, and she told me that she had followed this rude, mouthy boy underneath the bleachers because of what she'd heard him say about Amber. She had grabbed him up by the nape of his neck and threatened to beat the crap out of him if she ever heard him call her sister anything else. After we made it home that evening, Amber got to hear about all the excitement that Buffy had caused underneath the bleachers. Now, count it. Amber was at cheerleader "strike two" now.

The third and final straw happened one afternoon when I was about ten minutes late for picking her up from one of her many after-school practices. I drove up next to the school and there sat Amber on the curb just shaking and crying out like someone had just broken her heart in two. I got her into the car and asked her to tell me what had happened at cheer practice. She explained that one of the "meaner" moms had the duty of passing-out the school cheerleader sweaters. She patiently sat there as the lady called each cheerleader's name out to come forward to retrieve their new sweaters. Amber had remained silent until all the sweaters had been handed-out. She walked up in front of the entire group of girls and several of the mothers, and asked why she didn't get her sweater. She tried to let the woman know that she was certain that her mom (me) had already paid for the sweater. Finally, in a loud, bragging voice the mom in charge spouted back at Amber, "Well, to tell you the truth, we couldn't find a sweater big enough to fit you." Some of the girls then laughed out loud at the mom's words, and Amber had run out of the gym crying. She had been sitting there for ten or fifteen minutes crying over the way the mom had humiliated her in front of everyone.

Let's just say that I spent the next hour or so looking for the lady that had upset my child in such a disrespectful manner. It's probably a very good thing that I didn't find that woman that afternoon, or else I might have had a jail sentence added-in to my life experiences. To quote my beloved mother, "If you know what's good for you, then don't mess with my kids!"

That was basically it ---- "strike three" for the cheerleading. At home I point-blank asked Amber if being a cheerleader mascot was "fun". It certainly didn't seem like it was fun to me. I challenged her to really think about quitting her effort with this group of mean girls and even meaner moms. I boldly told her, "If this activity doesn't make you feel good about yourself, then drop it. It's just not worth it." A few days later she made the decision to chunk the mascot thing. And YES, she was right in quitting in the middle of the football season. If something doesn't build you up, then leave it behind and find something else that does. **No one, not even a child, should have to tolerate toxic people in life.**

On down the road the sport of tennis became the catalyst of Amber's extraordinary dose of self-esteem. She funneled most of her time and energy into her tennis lessons, school meets, and outside U.S.T.A. tournaments. During the ten or so years that she competed, she sometimes would hear some of her competitors whisper amongst themselves, "Oh, boy! I get to play the fat girl next." It was so satisfying for Amber (and me) when she would whip these girls all over the court. It was just such sweet justice in her sport.

Upon graduation from high school, her tennis coach helped her parlay her talents into a partial scholarship opportunity at Tarleton State University in Stephenville, Texas. And this very ambitious young woman's early college days' prediction came true........ She had always wanted to be a part of a college sorority, and her biggest dream (at the time) was that she would somehow get herself voted into this university's "homecoming court" as one of their popular queens.

When Amber was a Senior at TSU in 2000, she attained her goal of being voted onto the "Queens' Court" at the halftime of the homecoming football game. This was largely in part due to her affiliation with her Delta Zeta sisters. We were so very proud of Amber, and I'll never forget her words of encouragement to others that might be overweight and wanting desperately to fit-in, no matter what size they happened to be....... She confidently exclaimed, "Chalk "ONE" up for the fat girls of the world. It is possible and it can be done!"

Amber didn't win the Homecoming Queen, but given the fact that Tarleton State is a pretty good-sized university, it was quite a high honor for her to be selected to the court. It truly was a good day to be a fat girl, and an even greater day to be a fat girl's fat mother!

CHAPTER 16

What Goes Around Comes Around

After only two and a half years since my gastroplasty surgery, I slowly began stretching out my "thumb" stomach. At least, that was what the doctor had called my new baby stomach.

I think it all goes back to the fact that a big part of my overeating disorder stemmed from my psychological problems. Many times, in my past I ate because it made me feel good, or it kept me from boredom, or it calmed my nerves when I was anxious. Sometimes I had the privilege of eating because I was being rewarded for doing something good, and it always seemed to be a big meal or a special food treat for payment. I even remember losing several pounds after a good, successful week of being on the Weight Watchers program, and what would my mom do to celebrate with me? You guessed it, we'd go out and eat something fattening like Mexican food, and thus, this insane thinking probably put a couple of pounds back on me instantly.

I also blamed a lot of my overeating trouble on the fact that I simply adored food, both then and now! I didn't just eat fast food, or fattening food, or partake of too many sweets and such. I actually love all kinds of food – not just meat and potatoes and bread. I also enjoyed nutritious things like broccoli, squash, tomatoes, lettuce, bell peppers, carrots, sweet potatoes, and my favorite veggie of all time – any kind of onion. Unlike a lot of obese people, I usually ate very balanced meals. My downfall was the fact that I couldn't control my portion sizes. I would almost always go back for second helpings if they were available. I didn't feel like I was completely full until I left the dinner table in a state of misery. I often ate so much that I made myself sick. And that, in itself, is some sort of a twisted mindset, don't you agree?

Additionally, I blamed a lot of my weight gain on the Band-Aid fix that the gastro doctor tried to do on me. Basically, they wheeled me in, went through with the extreme surgery, and then sent me back home with a pat on the back and the good wishes of "Go home and be skinny". Well, that didn't seem to work for this fat girl. If I had known how to be skinny, then I probably wouldn't have gotten up to around 300 pounds in the first place.

Also, I had trouble sticking with the small portions when I ate after the surgery. I would look at the size of my new meals, and just know in my brain that I was not having enough to eat. But in the real world, I'm sure I was getting plenty of nutrition; I just wasn't getting the vast amount of food that my body was used to craving in previous years. I just kept on stretching and expanding my stomach over the next couple of years, until I finally forced the staples in my stomach to open back up, and I was right back to "square one".

After analyzing the debacle of my first surgery, I think the Lord just let me "fail" at my weight-loss procedure, mainly because I didn't want to lose weight for the right reasons. I was completely enthralled about looking better and changing my life options. At age twenty-five, I simply was not trying to lose the weight for improved health. Instead, I was selfishly trying to teach my husband a lesson of sorts.

You see, when you are extremely overweight, and particularly when you're a woman, you sometimes feel trapped in your relationship and/or marriage. It's like you wake up one day and realize that you have no real other alternatives in life. Because of your size, you are chained to the person that may have made the bad decision to marry you. Since Don and I were starting to have some serious marital problems, I desperately desired for the surgery to work so I had more available options in life. What I really wanted was to make him see was that if he didn't straighten his act up, then I would be armed with a smaller body and I could actually find someone else that would treat me better. As it stood, as long as I was fat and miserable in my marriage, basically I had no other options. So, when I started gaining all of my weight back, I was exactly back where I started before my surgery. A lesson learned the hard way due to my inability to handle myself as a much smaller person.

Returning were the old feelings of insecurity, the Fatty Patty voices in my head, and my general lack of confidence was becoming part of my personality once again. Back where the fears of walking across a crowded room, of boarding a plane and feeling like I was sitting on the passenger next to me, the uncomfortable experience of attending a sporting event, theatre, or concert where I had to cram myself into a too-small seat.

I recall one specific flying experience where I so very indiscreetly tried to ask the flight attendant for an extender belt since I couldn't fit into the regulation safety belt. Not to draw any attention to my big fat self, I had purposely called the busy attendant over to my seating area and very quietly asked him for a seat belt extension. He said, "No problem", so, I assumed that he would return momentarily and hand me the apparatus somewhat considerately. So, I waited and waited and waited.....and it appeared that we were about to take-off. The pilot had completed the taxiing of the plane to the point of waiting for clearance from the tower. By this time, I was sweating bullets, as the flight attendants were just about to get strapped into their special jump seats.

At the very last moment, I signaled one of the attendants that I still needed my extender belt. This extremely slim, young lady then stood at the front of my section of seating, reached down and pulled out the extender, held it up for me to see. She then asked me if the extension was what I needed, and then very nonchalantly tossed it back a few rows for me to catch. Well, well. That was certainly thoughtful of her. NOT! Probably only 20 or 30 of the people in my section got to enjoy that little flurry of embarrassment with me.

I also hated flying because of the close proximity of the passengers in the seating area. Inevitably, I always got the middle seat, which made me all-the-more comfortless during the flight, as I literally had to scrunch-up as best I could to keep parts of me from spilling over onto the person sitting on either side of me. I was totally exhausted by the time my plane touched down at the appointed destination. I had spent an hour or two in a pinched position, with no ability to relax and enjoy the flight.

If I had to fly long enough for a meal to be served on board, it was even more treacherous. The lap tray could not be placed down flatly over my mid-section, so there was no real way to put the food tray down in my lap like other passengers. Instead, I had to sit up and pull forward to hold the tray in place with my legs up to balance the food that way. All in all, my flying experiences always left me tired and frustrated and defeated.

Becoming more disheartened with the return of my larger body, I made a decision to try something brand new in the weight-loss field. One of our friends from church was a huge, heavy-set guy lovingly called "Flash". To explain, he was a big, rotund man with the sweetest personality ever. Despite his size, he was quite proficient at a wide array of sports --- tennis, softball, football, etc. His only drawback was his ability to run. He ran so slow that the nickname of "Flash" just stuck, and that was what everybody at church called him.

I so admired Flash because his weight never kept him from trying to do anything that he wanted to attempt. One summer Don and I were playing in a church coed softball league with him, and I kept noticing that he was dropping a huge amount of weight. Finally, I got up the nerve to ask him how he was losing so many pounds and inches, and I also wanted to know how he was doing it so quickly. "Hypnosis", he simply responded. He said he would gladly give me the business card of the clinic where he had been so successful.

A couple of weeks later I was ushered (or "herded", as in a large group of people which somewhat resembled "cattle") into an immense room. There were rows and rows of comfy recliners, and the finishing touch was the sound of ocean waves piped-in to set the mood for our hypnotic session about to begin.

I couldn't help but chuckle to myself at the comical scene I had quickly become a part of. All I saw around me were extra-wide recliners filled with overweight people seeking miraculous results to become "smaller" people. "Good luck with all of that", I quietly thought to myself.

A few minutes later, and the lights began to dim. A man's low, melodic, recorded voice pierced the silence with his rich, mellow sports announcer-type speech. The ocean background sound and music intensified as the deep "Voice" urged us fatties to relax and let go of our inner subconscious. That sounded quite inviting to the naked ear, but my very independent and in-control-of-myself inner person was all the while arguing with the recorded man's voice and his suggestions to let my inhibitions go.

The inner "Fatty Patty" kind of wanted to be put "under", but it was not going to happen. The "Voice" kept having us visualize being at rest on a beautiful sandy beach, with the ocean air blowing gently against our faces. He next suggested that we mentally "see" a waiter coming toward us with a large bowl of fresh, green salad. He enticed us to "want" the green salad, and not the high calorie pizza.

The "Voice" told us, "You no longer want to eat the pizza. You now crave the salad".

My inner self retorted defiantly back, "No. I still would choose the pizza. Sorry."

So, after about an hour's time had passed, my subconscious was still arguing with this very persuasive "Voice". I still never was able to obtain a hypnotic state of mind. I think I had basically just wasted my fifty dollars for something that seemed like nonsense to me. It might have worked well for Flash, but not for Fatty Patty. Count yet another failed weight-loss attempt that went ironically belly-up.

My family so enjoyed our pro sports as part of our lives, but the bigger I got, the more trouble I had fitting in the seats to enjoy the action in person. Be it ice hockey or football or basketball or soccer, or baseball, my big rear end just didn't seem to fit into the cookie-cutter seats. Maybe these seats fit the "average" American tush, but I seemed to have the over-sized caboose variety and I certainly was not "average" in any form or fashion.

I also thoroughly enjoyed going to music concerts. I remember one night very vividly, because I was miserably crammed-into my seat, totally uncomfortable, and I must have been sitting there with a terrible frown on my face. One of the ushers noticed my disdain, and came to my rescue. She suggested that my group of ladies might want to move up a few rows to the handicapped section where there were free-standing folding chairs available. That was such a sweet and kind thing to do for me. After the suggested move, I relaxed and enjoyed the show and was comfortable, too. What a nice treat! And the usher made this happen without embarrassing me in any way.

Over several years of marriage, I ascertained that Don's dream vacation always related to sports. One spring we planned a weekend get-away to Houston, Texas, about four and a half hours away from home. My parents kept our kids for the weekend, and so our fantasy trip included a Friday night minor league hockey game and a Saturday night pro basketball game at one of the city's best venues.

At that time "The Summit" was a great state-of-the-art sports complex. You entered the arena at the top and then proceeded to your seats by descending the stairs. We had primo seats both nights, so we had a long walk down the stairs until we located our ticket's final destinations. We were thrilled with the close-up view of the games' action, but my only fear was having to walk up all of those dreaded stairs at the end of the evening. Generally, stairs and I didn't get along too well.

Don and I thought it was amazing to see how they transformed the ice hockey rink back into a basketball floor so quickly. Also, one of the star attractions of the facility was the huge, raised big-screen, a predecessor to today's jumbo-trons.

On our final night in Houston we were enjoying the basketball game, but really getting a kick out of the way the cameramen found random people in the stands and then made fun of them on the big screen. Something simple like a person crossing his leg became funny when the camera guy would replay the leg motion back and forth, back and forth, to make everybody laugh.

It was getting late in the game, so Don decided that we should try to slip-out early to avoid some of the crowd. That way, perhaps we might miss some of the traffic jam at the conclusion of the sports event. I drew in a deep breath and turned to start my ascent up the long way to the top of the arena.

We had made it about half way up the steep stairs, when I had stopped briefly to try and catch my breath. About this time Don whispered into one of my ears, "Don't look back now, but the camera guy has your bottom on the big screen and he's making it bounce up and down in fast motion."

"Oh, my goodness! I've gotta get out of here right now." So I took off running up the stairs as quickly as possible. By the time I reached the top landing and turned to step into the lobby, my breathing was so labored that I was afraid that I was about to have a heart attack.

Then, after a few more minutes of trying to catch my breath, I looked over at Don and he was grinning from ear to ear like a Cheshier Cat. He quietly leaned over and said, "I was just kidding. You didn't have to take me so seriously."

One of these days I'm probably going to kill this man after one of his famous stunts like that! Well, on the positive side, at least he got me out of the arena quickly and we did beat the traffic out that night!

When our girls were teenagers we thought of a what appeared to be an economical and wonderful way to spend a hot, humid, summer day. We loaded up the car and drove to the Brazos River, about two hours away in central Texas. We rented tubes, brought our floating lunch in an ice chest, and set off on our first ever tubing adventure.

Often times in our State, the rivers and lakes get alarmingly low when we endure a season of little or no rain during the summer months. Such was the case during this specific year. We should have probably researched and read a little more about the art of tubing and noted the extreme drought conditions that we were experiencing first-hand in this memorable excursion as we floated down the Brazos River.

Because there was really no movement of the water and no wind to aid us, we were forced to use our own arms to create a current to keep us on course. After about thirty minutes of paddling with our arms as oars, we discovered that we had already chapped our fat arms, from our pits to our elbows. (At this stage in our family's life, the four of us were all overweight and feeling the same terrible discomfort.)

SPECIAL NOTE TO FAT PEOPLE TRYING THEIR HAND AT TUBING: Do not attempt this water recreational sport if you are overweight! The entire lot of us deeply regretted our decision to go tubing after about the first hour into our journey.

One thing about being overweight is that a person generally is much lighter in water. But that still doesn't help much when you have a heavy rump that drags and gets caught on every large rock in the river. Needless to say, our behinds were getting scraped and bruised beyond recognition with each and every bump that came our way. Sometimes the water was so low, that we would get caught-up in some tree stump roots, and one of our family members would have to drift over to rescue the other one from going aground.

You see, there were selected drop-off and pick-up points along several designated places down river. We were instructed that we could leave the general tubing course any time we desired to depart, but we simply had to swim to the chosen point where the shuttle buses were located.

We kept looking everywhere for these afore-mentioned pick-up points, but couldn't seem to find any of them. About five hours into this fun-filled adventure, we were chapped, bruised, and severely sunburned. We had already eaten our lunch a couple of hours back, so we were getting hungry again with all of the unexpected exercise. There was no food left, just the ice chest itself that we had attached to Don, along with an extra tube that we had tied to him earlier in the day. By now he was laboring to keep up with us, as we had weighed him down with the additional items that we didn't need anymore.

Praise the Lord, Amber and I finally spotted a shuttle bus on the east side of the river and we swam pell-mell to the shore with all of our energy that we could muster. Buffy was trailing behind us a little ways back, but where had Don disappeared?

We realized that he was waving his arms and he appeared to be struggling in the water. Buffy pushed her tube toward us and reversed her motion to start swimming toward her dad in rescue mode. He had so much stuff attached to him that he was literally about to drown. Amber and I were laughing hysterically on the shore, and we would have helped him, too, if we would have been able to catch our breath from all of the laughing. Buffy turned-out to be the hero of the day, helping her dad to the east shore where the bus was waiting for the four exhausted fatties.

It is a well-known fact that the Hulletts never do anything in a typical fashion. Anything we attempt usually ends up as a forever-to-be-shared story. The tale of us fatsos tubing is one of our favorite stories to contribute to our family's legacy of fun. There is never a dull moment with this family.

It was about this time that I had an unpleasant encounter, another bad "fat moment", with an animal, much like the case of "Buffy and the Dead Horse".

My husband's advertising firm was hosting their annual employee party, and this year it was being held at a fancy, dude ranch south of the Dallas area.

Instead of the usual formal-type parties and the photographer's "8 x 10" photo of each couple all dressed to the nines, we were advised to don western apparel like cowboy shirts, jeans, and boots. It was to be a bona fide wingding in a Texas-style setting, with us dressing in Texas duds, and we were served a delicious Texas barbeque dinner.

The photo opportunity this year was to sit on the back of a real-live, doped-up, over-medicated bull, this in staying in line with the country theme of the party.

I had already been asked several times to get on the bull for my annual picture, but I wasn't wanting to be a part of this exciting scene.

We thoroughly enjoyed the band, and we even danced to some of the good, country music. Later in the evening, we even learned a couple of line dances. (Well, I did. Don was not big on line-dancing at all.)

Don and I were having a lovely evening together, but the Human Resources lady kept pounding on me to get my photo taken with the zoned-out bull. She even tried to make me feel guilty, saying they had wasted their money on the bull pictures, as hardly anyone had chosen to get aboard the large, lethargic animal.

Finally, Don told the H.R. lady that we would appease her. He went first and everything seemed fine. Next, it was time for my big self to be hoisted upon the bull. I was carefully adjusting myself in the saddle, when the huge animal started relieving himself, probably because the great amount of extra weight that was just added to his back.

The results were all kind of noises, the most godawful excrement I had ever smelled, and one of the most embarrassing moments of my life!

Just like Buffy, I told them I wasn't good with animals – and I wasn't lying.

CHAPTER 17

The Rise and Fall of the Empty-Nesters

As the years went by, I matured and finally had accepted the fact that I was destined to be overweight. In the mid to end of the 80s I wrote another similar book called *"Fatty Patty"*, but I never pushed much to get it published. I just wasn't comfortable or happy with the ending. My acceptance of being extremely overweight and it being "OK" with me, just didn't seem the right way to summarize all my futile attempts at weight-loss. My "unsuccess" seemed like such an injustice to myself.

The never-ending fat stigma still was in place in my life, even as a new grandmother at age forty. When our first "grand" had some sort of stomach virus that left her with a high fever and nausea at age two, I rushed our little Kaylee to the pediatrician, and her mother met us at the doctor's office.

I went on to tell the lady physician that we were so worried about Kaylee because she hadn't been able to eat anything for a couple of days. We were also concerned because we felt that she might be dehydrated.

Much to my surprise, the doctor didn't seem to be very anxious at all about our toddler's condition. In fact, she began lecturing me about my negative impact on our rather "thin" little Kaylee.

This rude pediatrician's words cut like a knife, and I still remember the entire scenario today, after almost twenty-five years later. She tried to make her point by telling me, "Look, grandma. Your granddaughter will eat when she gets ready to eat. Please don't try to force food on her. After all, you don't want her to look like you, do you?"

And so, my hurtful "fat stories" continued to penetrate my life. The years went quickly by, and now my oldest daughter had kids of her own. I was enjoying being a grandmother, not to just one, but to four wonderful granddaughters.

Since both of our kids were finally out and on their own, Don and I made the huge decision in 1999 to move much closer to our 9-to-5 jobs, just north of Dallas. We thought we were making a good, solid business decision to save gas and to add some extra hours to our weekdays, especially since we wouldn't have to sit in rush-hour traffic any longer.

We first spent a year trying apartment living. It was ok at first, but a rather constrictive way to live after being used to residing for years in a single-family detached house of our own. We didn't find the noise level, proximity of neighbors, quantity of unattended children, etc., conducive to our regularly-patterned lives. Another negative thing was that I personally did not like having to make the trek down south every weekend so we could visit the kids and grandchildren.

One sunny Saturday morning in the last week of May in 2000, I was driving myself down the southbound highway to visit our families. I was suddenly distracted by a huge yard sale sign pointing toward a gymnastics facility. So many of our little granddaughters liked to dance and tumble and such, that I was confident I would be able to find some different-sized leotards and cheerleading paraphernalia that they would enjoy. I quickly exited the road and made my way to the busy sale in progress.

It was already heating-up on this bright spring day, so I had my dark sunglasses on. I kept moving along from display table to the next; however, someone had placed one of the tables over a disabled parking space. When I stepped back away from the display in front of me, my foot must have hit the unlevel raised part of the handicapped space and I went tumbling to the ground. The pain was so intense that I saw black in front of my eyes and almost totally passed-out.

Several of the gymnastic people came rushing to my aid, but the damage had already been done. My left foot and ankle were already swelling as I lay there on the concrete in the Texas noon-time heat. A couple of nice gentlemen tried to help me get upright, but I told them I was OK, that I just needed to sit there for a few more minutes to get myself together. I didn't want them to know how desperately I wanted to cry because of the extreme pain.

I next glanced around and realized that there were no handicapped parking signs or any other type of warning that would indicate the sloped area that I had stumbled on. A few more minutes of resting and I finally got myself back up and limped on to my car.

On to the first daughter's house I traveled, despite the surprise injury and mounting pain that was overtaking me. I tried my best not to dampen anyone's plans for the family to attend the City of Ennis' National Polka Dance at the largest Czech hall in town that evening. As we all met at the huge dance facility, I found myself a great spot where I could be a permanent spectator for the event. I simply loved watching those couples dancing to the happy polka tunes played by the Czech bands.

But by nightfall I had propped my leg up on another chair because the terrible throbbing action had started. I was miserable there on that Memorial Day weekend, but all I could do was sit there pretending that everything was OK. One thing for certain, was that I would not be joining any of our group on the floor that evening. There would be no dancing for me that night!

By the time we got home, it was well after midnight. I was totally exhausted and needed to bathe and then get right on to bed. I was confident that my injury was not a sprain. With all the throbbing I felt, I was about ninety per cent sure that I had broken a bone in my foot or ankle. Unfortunately, I would not be able to get in to see my doctor until Tuesday, the day following the Memorial Day weekend.

I limped on in to my primary physician's office, and just as I had feared, he took initial X-rays and then referred me on to a foot specialist, especially since I was so heavy. A couple of more days passed before I could get into the foot doctor's office. That morning I was already worn-out from just commandeering the steep stairs at our apartment complex and then dragging on in from the parking lot. The guy surveyed my X-rays of my foot and ankle areas, but the he diagnosed me with only a sprained ankle. He said because of my size, I would probably be better off in an orthopedic boot, so we went on to the local drug store to pick-up my new left shoe-bootie.

I thought this would be a quick in-and-out thing, but I guess I should have realized that nothing in my life seemed to be normal and pain-free. Of course, they didn't stock a boot big enough to fit my large calf. Now, we had to go to a specialty pharmacy place to order my extra-large size shoe-bootie. That meant walking around a few more days without any protection for my injured lower limb.

When the store called me, and let me know that my boot was in, I was surprised that the apparatus went from just under my left knee – down to almost the tip of my toe. What a way to spend a long, hot summer in Texas. I was to keep the huge boot on for three months and then come back in to see the doctor for a follow-up visit in mid to the end of August.

I was not going to be a happy camper in Texas for sure. Unfortunately, I was not going to be able to swim or do much of anything for at least ninety days. It was also a treacherous thing for me to drive with this crazy thing on my leg, too, but I somehow persevered. Some days it was all I could do to just hobble down our staircase, then drag myself to my car, drive myself to my job, and then slowly make my way back home and up the dreaded stairs at my place by late afternoon. By the end of most days I would be completely exhausted and worn-out. It was a royal pain lugging around over 300 pounds of dead weight on an injured ankle.

When it was time to go back for a revisit, the regular foot doctor was on vacation. I had to see another physician, and that turned-out to be a great thing. When I came lumbering-in, the younger man could tell from my face that I was still grimacing in pain. He immediately thought I should be passed this stage of healing after almost three months. He asked if his partner had ordered any X-rays of my foot and ankle when I first came in at the end of May. I told him "no", that my primary physician had sent me with his original X-rays. However, I informed him that my doctor's machine was rather antiquated and, per my doctor, he had me mention that his results might not be completely accurate. His partner had looked over the first doctor's results, but didn't think that I needed further X-rays done.

Well, this new doctor wanted new X-rays right away, so they marched me on down the hall for more testing. Sure enough, just like he figured, my ankle had been fractured all along, and now he was exceedingly concerned that I had walked around (at my size) on a broken ankle for three months. He told me that he was amazed at the level of pain tolerance that I must be able to bear. He literally couldn't believe that I would be able to endure that much discomfort with me being well over 300 pounds.

So now I was to continue wearing a more limited-motion type of leg bootie cast for a couple of more months, and afterwards I would soon start physical therapy for further rehabilitation. I carried on with following my foot doctor's orders, but the healing of my ankle was not coming along as well as expected. In fact, as a last resort, he prescribed a stimulus machine that sent small electric shocks into the fractured part of my foot. I wore this aggravating contraption to bed every night for weeks and weeks. Finally, my ankle healed and life went on.

However, because my first foot doctor had misdiagnosed my problem and because of all the other unexpected medical costs and time lost from my job, I decided to sue the gymnastics place where I had fallen. I had misplaced my foot on the curved handicap ramp that was not properly marked in their parking lot. I didn't know if I would get anything much out of my lawsuit, but I felt I was entitled to some small compensation from all the pain and trouble I had encountered because of their negligence.

About the same time Don had gotten a wonderful paying job at Electronic Data Systems ("EDS"). This mega-data company was formerly owned and operated by Ross Perrot. We were in the middle of negotiating a house deal in Lewisville, a city northwest of Dallas, and it would put Don much closer to his new job. Our main delay was gathering the amount of cash needed to be used at our upcoming closing. We were simply running out of time to move forward with the deal, and the settlement phase of our lawsuit just kept getting pushed back further time after time. We were at the point of pulling the plug on our closing date when the gymnastic studio's insurance company called us into their office to negotiate a fair agreement between both parties.

A close friend of mine was a mortgage attorney and she was trying her hardest to give us some good advice on how to negotiate and get the most money possible. First, she told us not to get our hopes up, that usually they will not extend an offer and pay-out in a cash settlement the same day. She also warned us that we probably wouldn't get any amount near the figure we had discussed privately with her, especially since we were going into the meeting without legal representation.

Regardless of all the negative feedback we had been given, Don and I continued to pray for God's will in this matter. In fact, if we didn't get a certain sum of money TODAY, then we would not be able to purchase the house that we wanted so badly.

The Lord must have been on our side, because we walked out of the insurance place with cold hard cash in hand that same afternoon. It was a couple of thousand dollars short of what we had anticipated, but it covered our initial down payment --- almost down to the exact dollar of what was required. Our God often shows up in a situation right on time.

Life seemed exceedingly good in the year 2000. My husband Don really liked his new job, and he was making the most money he had ever made in his life. In fact, I had a wonderful job at a large mortgage company in the Dallas area and had found myself in a good working position as well. I, too, was making a nice salary, this time in the mortgage banking business.

For the first time in a long time, we were in a house of our own, no longer renting, and finally enjoying the true American dream. It was so odd for me not to have to rush my check to the bank for deposit. In fact, sometimes I didn't have to cash my check right away at all. I began to save a little money and even used a portion for what I called my "play money". That meant that I got to go shopping for my kids and grandkids, and sometimes I even bought a little something for myself.

We were enjoying the prosperity so much, that it almost seemed like a dream. Don and I had struggled so many years of our marriage with finances, that it was like we were afraid that we might wake up and realize that the lives we were leading were nothing but an illusion. At this stage in my life, I tipped the scales at my highest weight ever --- a whopping 340 pounds. I know the increased weight-gain was a direct result of us eating out a lot more and splurging since we had extra money for the first time in our lives.

Then came the "9-11" terrorist attack in New York City in the fall of 2001, and "our" world came tumbling down, along with the "twin towers". The stock market plummeted and many businesses began to fall-apart with all the uncertainty surrounding that day and time. Before we realized what was going on, Don was facing a possible lay-off. The first wave of 5,000 employees was let go at EDS in the early part of 2002. A few months later and another 5,000 people were given their walking papers. About the time that Don was finally told that he would be laid-off in November (along with another 5,000 people), we were trying to brace ourselves for the possibility that he might be unemployed and would have to be forced to seek unemployment compensation while he tried to find another IT job in the already-crowded computer industry.

As we approached Don's lay-off date, we were delivered yet another crushing blow. I was surprisingly let go from my mortgage job, and I was told that I would not be able to draw unemployment insurance pay. Things were crumbling around us so quickly that we immediately put our house up for sale, and we were frantically trying to come up with alternative plans for living on Don's unemployment salary soon as our only means of income. That meant that we would be going from almost $100,000 a year of income, down to about $1,000 a month. No matter how we tried to analyze it, there was no way we could pay a house payment, utilities, three car payments, food, gas, etc. It just wasn't going to be enough for us to live on. Maybe Don and I would be able to find new jobs quickly, or at least, that was our early intention.

Then Don's final check arrived from EDS in November, and the reality of being jobless sent us both into a tizzy. It only took a couple of months without any real income for us to use-up all our limited savings. We had been so proud to send our daughter Amber off to college just a few short years previously. She was the first in our immediate family to go to college and come out with a degree. We tried to sell our house for about a year, but with no good success. The housing market was failing, too, and we finally had to let the house go back to the mortgage company. Next to go were the first two cars. They were repossessed, too, as we could no longer pay for them either. We were barely able to hold onto our one final car, but we didn't know how long that might last either.

We first moved into a tiny two-bedroom apartment near Amber, our youngest daughter. She was now newly-married and had quickly found a good, staple job right out of college. Her new husband was also gainfully employed. We, on the other hand, were sinking further with every passing day. We seemed to be making it ok the first couple of months, and then we got to where we barely had enough money for food. I remember those days of eating fried egg sandwiches for breakfast and then a lot of burgers and chicken sandwiches were served for lunch and dinner. It really didn't make any difference to me if I ate or not. I was so down and depressed that I hardly spoke to Don at all during the day. The big highlight of our week was getting in our car and traveling to the unemployment office. About the same time that Don had been laid-off from EDS, American Airlines, whose headquarters were based in the Dallas area, had let go a huge number of employees, too, so the job market was really flooded with people desperate for a job, any job. In fact, we made friends with a few couples like us, where both husband and wife were looking for jobs together. We would often see them again at the bi-weekly visits to the unemployment office. They would ask, "Any luck so far?" We would respond, "No. How about you guys?" And so, it would go, every time we made our jaunt to the government offices.

I prayed and prayed and prayed, but I didn't feel that God was listening to me at all. I kept crying out to Him, but it seemed that He had turned His face away from me. I became more and more depressed and bitter, even to the point of my health failing. I was unable to pay for my diabetes and other medications, so my body was on auto-pilot. It didn't seem to be reacting very well to the lack of prescriptions and the extreme depression and stress that I was putting it through. For a while my family physician was trying very hard to be able to supply me with the meds I needed by letting me come once a week to see what sample medications he might have available for me. This went on for a few months, but it finally got so humiliating that I was begging for samples, that I just gave up and altered my life to no longer worry about the prescriptions. I would have to make it somehow without the help of any medications until our financial situation improved.

This time was absolutely the lowest period in my life. I didn't even want to get out of bed every morning. I would sleep until eleven or twelve o'clock every day, make us a small brunch meal, watch my soap operas in the afternoons, make it through the evening meal, and then play Scrabble on the computer until two or three in the morning hours. That was what my life had been reduced to. Next, we were not even able to fully pay for our monthly apartment rent. Amber and her husband Boyd were now having to help us pay for our housing and buying some groceries for us, too. More depression followed, with no relief in sight.

About this time, Amber and Boyd found a nice three-bedroom house and moved away, so they could be closer to their jobs. Shortly thereafter, it was so painful to have to ask them if we could move in with them. We had financed our daughter throughout her college years, but now, only a short time later, we had to beg her and her husband to take us in and care for us, her parents.

It wasn't an easy transition, but we moved in as our last resort. In the meantime, I had several business associates that kept calling and checking-in with me about employment opportunities. One law firm in Atlanta, Georgia had continued to call me every couple of months. Their office manager, Georgia S., even asked if I would consider moving to Atlanta for a job. She promised that they would find a position for me within their firm. I told the lady that I certainly appreciated her offer, but there was no way that I could ever leave my family and friends behind in Texas. There was just no possible way.

Days somehow turned into months, and it had almost been a year since Don and me had been employed. We were now impacting Amber and Boyd's living conditions and marriage. We all knew that something had to give. So, I learned that you never say "never".

Summer was approaching, and one day I picked up the phone to hear the same law firm's appeal again for me to move to Atlanta. They generously offered to train me to become a title paralegal. I was extremely weak that day, so I finally discussed the proposition with my family. Don, more than anyone else, thought that I should give it a try. He encouraged me to take a step of faith.

This was absolutely the hardest decision I had ever had to make on my own. But after a lot of time and consideration and prayer, I packed up and Don then drove me to Atlanta, Georgia for a paralegal position that I never even had to fill-out an application for. They hired me right over the phone.

It was such a God-thing that I felt I had made the correct decision right away. We drove to our new life in Atlanta, almost 900 miles away, and four states to the east. I will never forget Don's face, as I kissed him goodbye and watched him disappear through the awaiting airport doors. Back to Amber's house he was going, and I was now all alone in a new place for the first time in my life. I had basically moved from my parents' house to Don's apartment in 1972 when we married, so I had never lived alone in my life. This was going to be a lot harder than I feared. My only help was going to be through my relationship with my Lord Jesus Christ. I was giving the entire situation all over to Him. Otherwise, I was never going to be able to make it on my own.

CHAPTER 18

Revival in the ATL

My new officer manager named "Georgia S." was the same one that had enticed me to make the big move to Atlanta. Upon arrival, she also helped me locate the cheapest place available, and luckily my "new home" would be in close proximity to the law office. There were not a lot of choices and I had started to work there at a lower salary than I had been making in Dallas. At this point in time, I just felt blessed to even have a job, so no griping from me was allowed. Also, my company benefits wouldn't kick-in until after being an employee there for three months, so I just prayed that my health would hold-up until I again had insurance and health benefits. Life without my prescribed meds was hard. I promised myself that I would schedule a full physical as soon as I had medical coverage again. Also, I was going to have to send money back to Don in Dallas every time I got paid. At the same time, my mother was having a hard time financially, so I knew I would have to mail her some assistance as well. Money was still going to be very tight and in short supply, but at least one of us now was employed.

After dropping Don off at the Atlanta airport, Georgia S. and I went off on our excursion to find me the perfect spot to live. The place she chose for me looked a little shady to me, but the price was what appealed to me at the moment. I moved in that very afternoon, walked across the street for dinner, and arrived back at my new home as the sky was turning dark. For the very first time, I noticed what looked to be prostitutes hanging around and, also, some drug dealer types lurking the area, too. I realized that I was going to be praying a lot in the coming days. God was really going to be busy protecting me in this scary environment.

I approached the door to my unit and it didn't look too secure. So just for grins and giggles, I took my shoulder and leaned hard into the door. Much to my dismay, the door opened right up without a key at all. It only took a good nudge to force the door wide-open.

My first night in my extended-stay hotel was not a very pleasant one. The hotel office said they could not send someone to repair my door until the next day. That meant very little sleep for me. I even propped a chair up under and against the door handle. Not that I thought the chair would keep anyone out, but instead maybe I'd at least hear someone if they tried to get inside of my room. (This always seemed to work in the movies, so I thought it might, at least, give me a tiny peace of mind.)

Hooray! I had lived through my first night away from home. The next morning, I got up for work, drove myself to the nearby law office, and started the training for my new profession as a title paralegal. The majority of the employees there seemed very nice and friendly. My trainer, Lee C., was very knowledgeable and helpful. Before long I was settled into a good daily routine. My real problems came at night when I was all alone and missed my husband, my daughters, and their families --- but especially my grandchildren. I would cry myself to sleep some nights. I also engaged in talking to myself in the large dressing mirror in my room. I guess I so needed to hear the sound of another human being, that I would literally talk to myself in the mirror like there was another person in the room.

"Where do we want to go for dinner tonight?", I'd ask my mirror person. She would reply, "Whatever you feel like will be fine with me". So, we'd freshen-up our make-up and either walk a short distance for a meal close by, or drive a few blocks for something more substantial to eat. However, some days I didn't have much money left before I'd receive my next paycheck, so I would have to just eat dry cereal -- whatever was "on sale" and cheap that week at the grocery store. Another first in my life was the feeling of not having enough to eat. As overweight as I was, I certainly wasn't starving, but it was just a new feeling of hunger that I had never experienced during my lifetime.

Those few first weeks were most definitely the hardest. I had a horrible television set in my room. I was only able to view about three different channels and the picture was still extremely fuzzy, to say the least. I often worked on my granddaughters' scrapbooks in the evenings. Pasting their pictures and writing funny captions in these memory books somehow made me feel closer to my girls. I didn't like to talk on the phone to them too much, as it just made me sadder to hear their voices. Most nights at the hotel I would watch a TV program or two before I went to bed at night around 8:30 or 9:00 p.m. I didn't know it at the time, but I realize it now, that the Lord used this extra time of rest to heal my broken body – both mentally and physically. There was also one other plus, and that was my king-size bed that was ultra-comfortable.

A few weeks later the law firm lady named Georgia S. also helped me in another amazing way. She invited me to her church, quite a way from the law office. She gave me directions and I made it around 9:30 a.m. for the morning worship hour at the local First Baptist Church of Snellville, the little town where she lived and raised her family. I looked all around, but didn't locate Georgia S. anywhere. This was a fairly, large church, so I could have easily overlooked seeing her. Discouraged to know that I would be sitting alone, I found myself a seat in the balcony area and settled in for a welcomed time of praise, worship, and teaching.

When it came time to welcome the visitors, a sweet lady behind me leaned over and shook my hand. She told me that she had seen me write on the Visitor Card that I was from Texas. She relayed that she and her husband used to live in Fort Worth, Texas, when he was attending seminary there. She introduced herself as "Georgia F." She asked if I wanted to join her for Sunday School after the worship service. Quickly I explained to her that another friend named "Georgia" was maybe going to meet me later. At the end of the service, she offered to help me find my friend so I could get to the correct Sunday School room. How uncanny that while living for such a short time in the State of Georgia, I had already met two nice ladies in person, both named "Georgia".

This woman, "Georgia F." was so kind and friendly that she walked me around the entire church campus, but we never could find my other friend named "Georgia S." She suggested that I just come with her, to her husband's class, and maybe I could connect with my friend the next week.

Well, these Georgia folks seemed to be very welcoming and they made me feel at home right away. I began coming to church every Sunday. And I finally found out that my law firm friend "Georgia S." never attended Sunday School at all. She chose to just attend the weekly worship service, so there was no way I would have ever found her in any of the classes there. God had somehow ordained that I would join the "Mark and Georgia Fite" Sunday School Class. And that is how my new life really began in Snellville, Georgia. The Lord had touched my heart and told me, "Patty, you are not alone anymore."

In fact, the town slogan for Snellville was, and still is today, "Everybody is SOMEBODY in Snellville". What a quaint, friendly, and welcoming little city this turned-out to be for me!

Some of the sweet ladies in my class invited me to join them in a "Ladies Night Out" which happened once a month. This was where a restaurant was chosen, and then we all met there for food and fellowship. This served as an excellent way to get to know each other. We could then understand how to best pray for and minister to each person in our group. This also helped me learn my way around the area, and I was beginning to feel much more a part of things. I was beginning to feel like I was somewhat a part of a family, since I was so far away from my own.

The day finally came around for me to get in to see a new local doctor. Surprisingly, they weighed me and I had lost 30 pounds without me really trying. I think the smaller meals and probably some of the past depression had contributed, but all the same, I was excited to have lost a chunk of weight. After one of our "Ladies Nights Out", I confided to one of my first Georgia friends, a very compassionate lady named Jane C., that I had gotten a pretty good clean bill of health earlier that afternoon. I told her about the weight loss and how I felt that God had used this alone time in Georgia to heal me from all my past ailments and lack of meds. The new doctor had even cut back the amount of diabetes medicine that I had been prescribed the year prior. I confessed that the only negative thing from my check-up was a small mass found in one of my breasts that was detected in my mammogram. Jane quickly decided to pray for me right then and there. Her prayer really calmed my nerves, and I felt much better after she told me that I shouldn't worry myself over it.

Jane turned out to be right. Another test three months later, and the mass seemed to be totally non-existent. The technician thought that there may have been a shadow on the first mammogram results, but I am more confident that it was the Lord and my friends' prayers that had healed my body yet again.

On down the road I made closer friends with another lady in my Sunday School class. Her name was Laura R., and she had a nice husband and three sweet daughters that played a lot of different sports. We had that natural connection of both having girls, and the sports thing kind of sealed the deal.

I heard her talking about her girls playing softball games during the week nights there in Snellville. I asked her for a schedule of their games. I certainly was not very busy every evening, so maybe I could drive to town to see some of their games. This fostered a life-long friendship that I still cherish to this day. It didn't take long until I became a sort of permanent fixture at the girls' games. I always tried to be there if I had the gas to make it. To me, it was so enjoyable to get outdoors in the evenings, and especially wonderful to get to be closer friends with the Rawson family of Snellville.

After a few months of being on my own in Atlanta, Don was finally able to save enough money for him to join me in my new place. He was astonished at how well I looked and he marveled even more at how I was handling myself in the metropolis called "the ATL". After a few hours of being with me again, he remarked, "I don't think you really need me anymore. Here you are in a new locale........you already know your way around in this very large and busy city, you're doing well at your new job, you've made friends, and you've even found a church that you love. Are you sure you still need me?"

The only negative thing Don had to share with me was his concern about the place where I was living. He, too, thought this hotel was what he considered a "flop house". He also noticed some of the shady-looking characters that were our neighbors. But as I told him, "I just pray a lot, and the Lord somehow sends His angels around to protect me."

As thrilled as I was with having my best friend with me again, we still had more difficult challenges ahead of us in the days to come. It was almost another year before Don found an IT job in Atlanta. This city, too, was experiencing lean times in the job market. There were tons of people looking for jobs and there just weren't many jobs to be found.

One Sunday at church, I was talking about the crazy hotel where we lived. My friend Laura R. chimed in and said, "Patty, come on. It can't possibly be as bad as you make it out to be. After church is over, I'll follow you to your hotel so I can judge for myself." Don and I agreed to let her follow us, but we kiddingly told her to roll up her windows and lock the doors of her car. After our 30-minute commute from the church in Snellville to our little town of Tucker, we safely arrived at our very humble abode.

I could see by the look in Laura's eyes that she couldn't believe what we were living in either. She started asking me how much we were paying a week to stay there. She admitted what Don and I had already realized, there was no way we were ever going to be able to save enough money to move somewhere else while we still had to pay the rather high weekly amount for the "dump" we lived in.

I could tell that her mind was at work trying to come up with a plan for us. All at once, she blurted out, "Let me talk this over with my husband, but I'm going to see if we can have you guys move into our sunroom at the back of our house. Then, you should be able to save the money you would normally pay for rent, and maybe use that cash to find a better place to live."

We could not believe the words that had come out of her mouth. At last, we had found a possible solution to help us get out of the hellhole that we were chained to. What a wonderful offer from a caring friend! The next week we were free to move out of our hotel, and we relocated to the city where our church was located, the place where "Everybody is SOMEBODY in Snellville". Laura and her husband Lloyd had graciously agreed to give this a try for two or three months. Hopefully, we would be able to save enough money to put a down payment or a deposit down for a new place for us to live. In the meantime, we were so enjoying the home-cooked meals and the feeling of being a part of a busy family, and with their three wonderful girls as an added bonus. About the same time, Don had finally secured an IT job in Atlanta. Things were finally starting to work out, or, at least, move in the right direction, for the Hullett family.

Laura would cook the evening meal and I would do the dishes, and then the next night I would cook and she would do the cleanup. We had good, long conversations at the dinner table every night, and we all shared funny stories from our past with each other. During these six or eight weeks with the Rawsons, life was extremely good for us. We had a nice, clean room of our own, and we had a TV that worked properly. Laura had even dragged an old recliner into the sunroom. It felt so great to be able to sit upright and watch a television program at night. I always had to lie down on my bed to watch TV at our famous "flop house".

Laura came in very excited one morning. She had noticed a "For Lease" sign at the two-story home right across the street from their house. Sure enough, we all walked over later that day and tried to peer in through the windows of the rent house. It appeared to be in good condition, and Laura took the initiative to call the phone number on the sign so we could take a real look inside of the home. A couple of days later the two guys that jointly owned the rent house met us at the site and unlocked the door for us.

We were so enthralled with the size and layout of the house. It was a beautiful home, with a large living room, formal dining room, kitchen, laundry room, and half bath located on the bottom floor. The back door opened onto a long screened-in porch, with a lot that was lined at the back of the property with stoically straight pine trees. These handsome pines provided wonderful shade for the back-porch area.

Another bonus was the front porch which included an over-sized porch swing hanging at the north end and it featured large picture windows. Upstairs there were three nice-sized bedrooms, and the master bedroom was especially huge. There were two full baths on this second story, as well as a bonus room above the two-car garage. Needless to say, it would work perfectly for us.

Now, if only the price would be something we could afford. And there was also the obstacle of talking the owners into giving us a chance to rent. After all we'd been through the past couple of years, our credit was ruined and they would have to be willing to give us a fair shot of proving that we could be excellent renters for them.

That is where Mrs. Laura really showed her spunk as our very own personal real estate negotiator. She kicked her personality into gear, and over the next couple of days, any time she saw the owners working at the house across the street, she made a beeline to where they were working and then made her presence known. She was relentless on these guys, letting them know that I worked for a large and reputable law firm, and that my company would direct deposit half of my monthly rent each time I got paid on the 15th and last day of each month. Nothing would be left to chance. As long as I worked for this law firm, they would get their rent money bi-monthly as scheduled.

Don and I never knew if Laura was that great of a salesman or if she just hammered the poor owners into submission, but she somehow managed to get the deal approved. It wasn't long into we were able to move into our new "empty" house, right across the street from the compassionate Rawson family. All our personal belongings, furniture, paintings, knick-knacks, etc., were still in a storage facility back in Texas. And that meant that we would have to come up with about $2,000 to get the things out of storage and then moved to our new home in Snellville, Georgia. Here we were with this big, spacious house to live in, but with no real household items of our own to turn this house into a real home.

CHAPTER 19

The Best Little Sunday
School Class in America

One of the ladies at my law firm (Georgia S. again) heard about our dilemma, and our good fortune to have a big house to live in. She immediately had Don come to her home and pick up an extra queen-size bed that no one was using. So, we were thrilled and excited to have our first piece of furniture in our new place. Laura also willed us the old, comfortable recliner that we had used in her sunroom, so things were looking up for us.

A few days later the Fite Sunday School Class arrived to literally furnish our beautiful home. The Fite family loaned us an older dining room table and chairs, as well as some table lamps for our living area. Another lady named Lisa came with a complete set of dishes, which I thought was kind of a God-thing, especially since I had adorned the exact pattern a few years back when I had the same ones in my home in Texas. Another couple brought a couch, another delivered some end and coffee tables. Our downstairs area was quickly filling up because of the generosity of our sweet Sunday School friends. And the class members who didn't have big items to donate offered other help with bathroom items and kitchen supplies. We simply could not believe the way this wonderful group of people took care of our every need. Thank you to the "Best Little Sunday

School Class in America" – part of the wonderful First Baptist Church of Snellville!

I was the queen of garage sales, so in the next weeks that followed I set about trying to locate our remaining household items in the second-hand manner. It wasn't too long until my oldest daughter Buffy and her family had made the trek to Georgia and wanted to live here, too. It was, for sure, that we had a big enough house for them to start out with us. Hopefully they would be able to find jobs right away and then maybe they could get a place of their own. Enter again the awesome church people. More beds were needed, so once again they stepped in to either loan or give us the extra beds for our extended family.

Amber, the other daughter, wanted us to move back home to Texas. She said that she and her husband were trying to get pregnant, and that Don and I would surely move back home if she was having their first baby. I finally told Amber that I did not want her to get pregnant. And it came true.

I was elated that I was able to get Buffy a job at my law firm, and she seemed to be happy with her new position. It wasn't too long before her husband found a job and they moved off to another town about 30 minutes away from Snellville. Her girls seemed to like the new schools and everything seemed to be rolling along quite well.

About a year later, childless and frustrated with not being able to get pregnant, Amber and her husband Boyd now joined us in the Atlanta suburb of Snellville. They lived with us for a while, and I talked my office manager (Georgia S.) once again into giving another one of my daughters a chance at the law firm. Amber was soon hired, so she joined Buffy and me at the same office.

Amber was so disgusted about not being able to conceive, that she begged me to join her in a local ladies' gym and exercise club. I didn't really want to go, but she can be very persistent and just beats you down. Before I knew it, she had gotten me to do what I never wanted to commit to. This was the case in our becoming a part of the local health club. The first couple of weeks almost killed me. I had not exercised in years and I was afraid I might just kill over with a heart attack during this type of strenuous circuit training.

We would first stretch, and then ride stationary bicycles for about ten minutes. After I got through with that, my legs felt like rubber, but we moved on to the jogging mat. We worked out while listening to the upbeat music and then the recording signaled us to move along to the next exercise machine. After the tone, we progressed to the step apparatus, and then moved on to the next machine, and then we jogged again, used the next machine, then used the step apparatus again, etc. We followed this circuit-training regimen for about a 45-minute total workout. After about a month, I had lost about 15 pounds and Amber had lost 25. And guess what happened next?

Amber went for a physical, and low and behold, her new doctor announced that she was pregnant. Amber had purposely kept it a secret from us for a couple of months until she had the news of the gender of the baby she was carrying. One day she came home with a little wrapped gift for us. Don had me open it up, and inside of the pretty little box was a blue angel teddy bear. We all looked around the room at each other, and I finally figured out what she was trying to tell us. Thank the Lord, we were going to be grandparents again and we were finally going to have the first grandson that we had all been waiting for. There were lots of hugging and crying going on, but as I reminded her previously, "I told you that you were not going to have a baby until we were all together again". Mama Bear (me) was right again!

So that ended Amber's obsession of going to exercise class 2 or 3 times a week, but for some strange reason I just kept on being a part of the group. I guess because it made me feel better, and I was making some new friends while we worked-out together. A few more months passed, and I had lost about 30 pounds and felt better than I had in years. I had also gone from wearing size 4X (size 30-32) clothing down to 2X (size 22-24). That might not make you think that was such an awesome feat, but to me, it was a paramount accomplishment. I could actually find some stylish clothes, and that made me feel much better about myself.

Don and I still didn't have much extra money after we paid our bills each month, but we tried to do what we could to help-out at our church. We wanted to give back by donating our time and service. Our tithe and other contributions were not great amounts, but instead we volunteered for everything that came down the pike at First Baptist. We felt so indebted to this giving group of people that we tried to give of ourselves as often as we could. We joined in the Fall Festivals where we worked games or handled the carnival rides as best we could. We helped with the Angel Tree packages and deliveries each Christmas. We gathered school supplies for needy kids at the beginning of each school year. We tried to support the youth group and their ministry opportunities. We even joined in some of the Wednesday night visitation groups. We were very actively involved with all our church ministries and activities. We were connected.

We particularly enjoyed the 4th of July celebrations with our church family. I'm almost certain that First Baptist Church – Snellville was one of the largest churches in our hustling and bustling little town. It was always a running joke among the FBC members, as the neighboring Methodist Church was across the street from our church – right on the main thoroughfare of our fair city.

Our church always proudly boasted and advertised about our First Baptist Church day-long celebration on the Saturday on or closest to the actual 4th of July. We were quite a lucrative church, so we could afford to put on quite a church-wide Sunday School Class picnic event, which ended the evening extravaganza with a monstrous fireworks display.

Much to our amazement, the Methodist Church would always seem to promo "their" fireworks celebration. But all they did was use "our" fireworks to promote their event. We would make good-natured comments about our church neighbors advertising "our" display!

We'd say things like, "You know those wacky Methodists can really be crazy sometimes." Then, we'd all get a big laugh out of the deal.

One July 4th was quite memorable, as we and some of our close Sunday School friends arrived on the church grounds early to set-up the tents and pop-up gazebo for our class meal planned later that evening. These camping aids were helpful in keeping the hot July sun off our class members.

About the time we were trying to get all our tent and gazebo items all assembled and placed on our assigned location on the church parking lot, there came, out of nowhere, a huge thunderstorm that hit us like a ton of bricks. The thunder was even more enhanced by the huge, towering pine trees all around the church acreage. And lightning strikes were prominent in that area. Because of the sandy soil and the trees not having much deep roots, heavy thunderstorms could prove even more dangerous, when trees were sometimes struck and then fell on unsuspecting bystanders or even on cars as they passed by the downed trees.

As we expressed previously, we loved our church with all our hearts – and we were willing to do almost anything to support this body of believers that had been so good to us. Therefore, that day we literally risked life and limb as the storms rumbled through our huge church property. We, along with 3 or 4 other faithful class members, stood there through all the torrential rain, wind, lightning, and thunder, just trying to protect our equipment. This meant that we were holding-up metal poles, while the slow-moving severe weather moved through our area. It was the loudest thunder and brightest lightshow we had ever experienced. Thankfully, we lived to tell about it.

We can honestly say that First Baptist Snellville was the most amazing and generous church that we have ever had the privilege of being a part of. And our volunteerism always blessed us more than the blessings we could give by helping.

In fact, one day our Sunday School teacher, Mark Fite, had inherited an older model Ford Crown Victoria from a deceased family member. I believe it was an aunt, as well as I can recall. We were dumb-founded when he handed us the car keys and signed-over the title to us so we could enjoy the luxury of having a second car. Can you believe the over-the-top generosity of these sweet Georgia people? Don and I have never seen the likes of God's people that gave without any hesitation. We will always have a special place in our hearts for these wonderful Snellville Christian friends!

The past few years that we had spent in the valley of depression seemed to curve upward now. We were planted securely in our new home, with new jobs, with new friends, and a new outlook on life in the great State of Georgia. I continued to get more physically and spiritually fit as our "valley" days seemed to be gradually turning into mountain-top experiences for us to look back at and marvel over in the years ahead. This was largely due to the agape love and mercy shown by our God, as well as by an extraordinary group of awesome Christian friends from the First Baptist Church in Snellville, Georgia.

CHAPTER 20

Back to My Roots

As much as we had enjoyed living in Georgia, the call of home came suddenly as we were completing four full years away from our native State of Texas. The oldest daughter Buffy and her family had moved back home the previous year, and in October of 2006 I moved on to a new law firm in the suburb city of Decatur, just a few miles outside of Atlanta.

Everything changed so quickly, as the youngest daughter Amber was offered a promotion by my original law firm in spring of 2007. Her agreement would ride on the invitation they offered her to move back to the Dallas, Texas area and to open a new eviction office there to service one of their large clients. Amber thought about the opportunity, the raise, and the promise of paid moving expenses if she and her family were willing to relocate. It didn't take much consideration on her part, and a few weeks later she, her husband, and their new baby boy were headed back to Texas.

I immediately approached my relatively new boss and told him my dilemma -- that both of my daughters and their families had now moved back home to Texas. This was a whole new ballgame, with the only remaining members of our displaced family now down to two -- my husband and myself. I gingerly asked the managing partner a very pointed question. "Have you ever considered letting anyone work from home before?"

I could tell he took an extra few seconds to ponder my proposal. At the time I was the only title paralegal that handled the bank-owned mobile home piece of the foreclosure business. He spouted back, "We've never really seen the need to let someone work from home." But he followed-up by telling me that he would think about the possibility and get back to me soon. Sure enough, after three days had passed, he walked into my office and told me that he would "OK" the proposed move back to Texas. He said that he would be willing to give this work-from-home attempt a try, and we'd see how it played-out.

After a few weeks of planning and winding down my title work at the Decatur, Georgia office, we found ourselves on the long road back to our home State of Texas. Amber had located a large rent house for all of us to reside in. In fact, she had found a lovely garden home that had never been lived-in previously. It was the model home of the part of the city of Midlothian in which we would now all be living together in. The four-bedroom brick home featured a beautiful front flower garden and was defined by a black wrought-iron security gate. In fact, the model home had previously included a two-car garage, but that space had been become a large study or extra bedroom, complete with its own heating and air conditioning unit.

The house seemed to work-out perfectly for us. Don and I had the larger furniture pieces so we took the master bedroom suite, Amber and Boyd took the next biggest bedroom, the new grandson Brendan occupied the smallest bedroom, and the remaining room was targeted to be my work-from-home office for my law firm. The large remodeled garage area now became inhabited by our teenage granddaughter Kaylee. She loved the privacy and having a new area of her very own. That was especially heart-warming to all of us older folks, as it was a godsend that we didn't have to endure her loud, incessant rap music.

Our intent was for us to stay together in this one large, five-bedroom house, as Boyd was beginning the process of re-enlisting into the Army. He and Amber had both received degrees from their university in 2001, but they were being hammered by student loan debts that kept mounting up after only six short years upon their graduation. Boyd decided that it would be better for him to go back into the military, where he had confirmed that he would be getting a grand total of $42,000 for re-enlisting and as a special signing bonus. That way, Amber and son would continue to live with us, while Boyd was away for a couple of years.

About the time things were coming together for Boyd's major shift back into military service, he was unexpectedly called away to be a part of his grandfather's funeral service in 2006. This sweet man (named Robbie) was an outstanding role model to Boyd and he was certainly going to miss his favorite grandfather. What he didn't know, but soon came to realize, that this wonderful man had left him a pretty large sum of money according to his will. And as the Lord worked it out for Boyd and Amber, the amount of his inheritance was none other than $42,000 -- the exact amount that Boyd was going to receive if he had made the final choice of re-enlisting in the army. Our God had blessed our family yet again.

No longer would Boyd have to worry about leaving his family to help cover his and Amber's college debts. His grandfather had given him the needed funds to take care of a large part of their college debt, and, also, there was enough left-over for them to take care of the down payment for a new starter house of their own. In a few short weeks, Amber, Boyd, and Brendan had moved away, but less than a mile away from Don, Kaylee, and me. The Lord was in the business of working-out things according to His plan -- again.

It seemed like in no time at all we were comfortably fitting into our old lives in Midlothian, Texas. It was great to be living closer to my mother again and it was so nice seeing old friends that we had so dearly missed while we were away for four years. No longer did I exercise, no longer did I go for walks, no longer did I watch what I ate, and no longer was I craving "real" authentic Mexican food like I did while in the confines of Georgia. I had to attest to the fact that Texas undoubtedly proudly boasts of having the best Mexican food north of the Mexican border. In fact, I would feel confident of saying that we have the best Mexican cuisine in the entire United States of America. Based on that fact, my appetite had returned with a vengeance. Here again I found myself looking at that terrible number of 300 pounds on my home scales. Exasperated and defeated again, Fatty Patty had returned home to her old way of unhealthy and unfit living, just like before.

It continued to work out well for me serving as a Georgia paralegal, even four states away. Things seemed to be fitting together quite nicely, and Don and I were both pretty fat and happy. However, in late 2009 and throughout all the year of 2010, I started encountering medical problems that I couldn't seem to pinpoint. My stomach problems really intensified by the time the year of 2011 rolled around. I was regularly having extreme cramping in my mid-section, I couldn't hardly sleep at night unless I sat-up in my recliner, I was often passing blood and had no idea of why. I kept putting off going to the doctor because I was afraid that I might have stomach cancer. I had also been losing weight without really trying. This worried me all-the-more.

In June of 2011 Don had to drive me to an appointment with a gastro specialist. It was becoming increasingly painful for me to make it through each day without severe symptoms. This very sweet African doctor told me that it appeared to him after my initial examination that I must either have stomach cancer or bleeding stomach ulcers. He confided to me that he and I should both join in prayer that my trouble would turn-out to be ulcers, not any type of cancer. In the meantime, he sent me on directly to the hospital down the street. He said that it was imperative that I get a couple of units of blood in me right away.

The doctor had the hospital keep me over night. The following morning, he came by to give me his test results. With him on his rounds, there was another doctor who was the internal surgeon. They jointly explained to Don and me their good news. It was true that I had a huge bleeding ulcer in my stomach; it was good that it was not cancer that we had worried about. However, the bad news was that the ulcer was about the size of a baseball. This meant that they would need to take about 70 percent of my stomach to remove the infected area. I certainly didn't want to undergo surgery at my age, but at this point I didn't see where I really had any other choice. In fact, the African doctor urged the surgeon to consider doing a gastro-bypass, while he removed a large portion of my stomach. He tried to rally the surgeon into rolling both surgeries into one operation. I don't think the surgeon was onboard with the two-for-one thinking, but my doctor brow-beat him into submission. He finally agreed to perform joint surgeries, if I would only consent to it.

Only nine months prior, Amber had undergone a relatively new weight-loss surgery (called the duo-denal switch) by a rather famous Dallas surgeon. She was his first patient to undergo that specialized surgery meant for someone that needed to lose around 200 pounds. Topping out at 340 pounds, Amber fit the bill for this extreme weight-loss surgery. In the short time after her October 2010 surgery, she had lost approximately the size of two people that she had been carrying around on her back all those years. All the family and friends that she encountered after the drastic surgery, were totally astonished with the tiny person she had become. Her total weight loss was now around 205 pounds. At her very lowest weight since around the fourth grade, she was tipping the scales at 135 pounds. This life-changing surgery had completely transformed her into a new and different person. She looked and felt absolutely wonderful. She encouraged me greatly to take the weight-loss chance that the Lord had presented me with. I guess I was just nervous about going through such a serious surgery at my age.

Don, on the other hand, seemed to be my main obstacle holding me back. He most definitely did not want me to have the surgery. He kept telling me what he had always told me over all our years of marriage -- that he "loved me just the way I am". And to a fault, that is how he held me prisoner of being an overweight and often miserable person for decades. As usual, he continued his non-support of my attempt to lose a drastic amount of weight. He held to the fact that he liked "fat" girls, not "boney" ones.

I prayed about this bad thing, the bleeding stomach ulcer, for several days and then realized that this surgery might be the best thing the doctor could have ever offered me. I literally was getting a chance to take care of my continuing stomach problems, while at the same time; I was being given another chance of living life at a normal, healthy weight. It seemed like my God was giving me an awesome opportunity to add years to my life once again. The chance was out there for me, if I were only willing to take it.

CHAPTER 21

Decision of a Lifetime –Desperate
Times Call for Desperate Measures

What is Gastric Bypass Procedure?

By AdminDr on March 21st, 2012
(from website – www.gastric-bypass.org)

"Gastric Bypass is a surgical procedure that assists the patient in losing weight by modifying how the stomach and small intestine digest and absorb the food you eat. Following the gastric bypass surgery, the stomach size will be smaller. The patient will feel fullness with simply eating less food."

"The food the patient takes will no longer go toward several regions of the patient's stomach and small intestine that digest and absorb food. For this reason, the patient's body will not take all of the calories from the food the patient consumes."

"Having gastric surgery is not risk-free though. People who have undergone this procedure would report more cases of gallstones, and in other studies, they would also report nutritional issues like anemia or osteoporosis."

"Every year there are about 140,000 gastric procedures being performed in the United States alone. The results could really be successful, with people being able to get better weight-loss results, however, about 2% of

patients would find it fatal. In the 2%, one percent could be as a result of complications during surgery. The heart is unable to support the pumping it has to do to handle the excess weight or the complication brought by it."

It took an immense amount of courage on my part to take the step of faith of a second, very serious weight-loss surgery. Not only was I fearful of something going wrong with the surgery at my age, but more than that, I was terrified to fail once again after another extremely intensive procedure to lose weight. There was no way that I wanted to strike-out again after being given yet another chance to finally obtain my lifetime goal of being a normal-sized person.

I wasn't asking to be the size of a super model or a movie star. I wasn't asking for the world. I just wanted to not have people stare at me in a restaurant or look at me when I walk across a room.

Because I had the unique situation of having an active bleeding stomach ulcer, the doctors agreed that I shouldn't take the normal time of going through the several-week regiment of drinking only liquids like clear broths and protein shakes to get my stomach ready for a complete lifestyle change. In fact, they rushed me through the standard testing in just a few short days.

First, I had to undergo an upper and lower G.I. series of tests to see what my stomach looked like since my original gastroplasty and staple surgery had taken place in the early 80s. Once they determined that I was an approved candidate, I immediately had to go through a thorough battery of blood tests.

From there, I was sent to a psychiatrist for a mental evaluation. This lady doctor and I really hit it off, personality-wise. She was rather heavy-set herself, so I think that she talked to me a lot more than her usual psychiatric evaluation patients. As a matter of fact, I told her of my desire to write my autobiography back years ago, but that I had failed in that attempt. She graciously offered her support of my endeavor to inform others of the many trials encountered because of being a morbidly obese person in this day and age.

My next quest was to visit a local cardiologist to check my heart and its ability to undergo this type of strenuous surgery. I also knew that I had to be able to pass a mandatory stress test. I rushed into the doctor's office early one morning prior to my surgery date. I hadn't bothered to eat breakfast that day, so they took me on back in their lab area to first draw some blood.

I was sitting there on a long, cushioned bench, waiting my turn for more blood tests. Suddenly, I felt faint, so I tried to tell the attendant that I wasn't feeling well. She brushed me off and told me to just sit back and relax. A few minutes went by and I tried to continue to alert anyone within hearing distance that I was about to faint, but no one came to my rescue.

The next thing I remembered was waking up in a kind of fog, and with a feeling like I was floating on a cloud. As I tried to re-adjust my eyes, I found myself surrounded with about ten men and women gathered around me, trying to get me to sit up and come-to. As I had told them, "I was about to faint" --- and faint was exactly what I did.

That even scared me even more, as I was afraid that I would not be able to pass the required stress test now. The staff made me sit upright for half an hour, before they would allow me to walk into the doctor's office for an interview with the cardiologist.

Because I had passed-out, they did not want to inject dye into my body for a nuclear stress test. This type of exam is done by using a radioactive tracing material that is injected into your bloodstream. This test is performed by comparing two pictures of your heart—one when the heart is stressed, and one when the heart is at rest.

Instead, they opted for me to use the exercise stress test. After the morning I had experienced, I was not confident at all that I would be able to walk long enough on the treadmill for them to get the results that the cardiologist needed.

I stepped up on the walking apparatus and tried to have a good, positive attitude about what I was to undergo. I started off well the first couple of minutes, and then I got into my huffing and puffing stage, and hung on in the last part of the test with my legs aching and burning. Truth be known, I had been able to stay on the treadmill longer than I had anticipated. And thankfully, I had somehow passed the doctor's requirement for my surgery.

Lastly, I had to attend health and nutrition classes a few days prior to my procedure. Sitting in a class with about ten other fatties in varying degrees of obesity, we listened and learned about the drastic surgery we were lined-up for. We were instructed on what we would have to eat or drink before and after the surgery. The nutritionist went through a workbook of data for us to be advised of, and then she held an open question and answer period at the end of each class.

I had been particularly impressed with the main lady instructor, as she had been a bariatric patient years ago, and she had continued to successfully keep her weight off years after her surgery. It was always more encouraging for me to hear and accept teaching from someone that had been in the same kind of shoes that I found myself in.

Once I had jumped through all the required hoops as proposed by my surgeon's office, they set about to determine the exact surgery date for my operation. I received a call back from them a few days later, and they informed me that the doctor would be going on a two-week vacation soon. He would not be able to schedule my surgery until mid-August.

I was heartbrokenly sad and found myself in the throes of deep depression. I did not want to wait for six more weeks. I didn't want to keep passing blood with the possibility of having to go into the hospital again for more units of replacement blood. I did not want to spend more sleepless nights where I would have to rest in an upright position in my recliner. I also did not think I could endure six weeks of the liquid diet and the protein shakes.

Being the persuasive writer that I can sometimes be, I sat down and penned a strongly worded letter to my doctor that was set to leave soon for his vacation. I almost down-right begged him to try to fit me in somehow BEFORE he left on his trip away from the office, and I sited all the reasons why I couldn't wait that long.

My plea must have done the trick, because he ordered his staff to work around his schedule to assist me and my situation. One of his nurses called me back with a slated surgery date of July 6, right after the 4th of July holiday weekend. I was so thankful that the doctor had a kind heart after all.

Monday, July 6, 2011 could not come soon enough for me. I felt this was my last real chance of achieving a significant weight-loss, and as a result, I was hoping to add some years onto my life. After all, I had been diagnosed with Type 2 diabetes in 2001 and had been on meds since then. Also, the bleeding stomach ulcer problem was a real concern.

Unbelievably, I somehow had good blood pressure, but on the down side, I was taking another drug for high cholesterol. Knowing all these personal medical conditions, I was finally ready and up for the challenge that lay ahead of me.

CHAPTER 22

To Be Fat or Not to Be Fat, That is the Question

I was up even before my alarm clock went off. I didn't sleep much, as I guess I was just too keyed-up (and worried) about a day that might (or might not) change my life forever. Don and I arrived at the hospital around 7:00 a.m. My surgery was set for 8:00 a.m. but we still had to check in, get settled, and then meet with the anesthesiologist.

I had to admit that I usually did not do well with any type of anesthesia. Prior, in my other surgeries, I always had the unpleasant experience of waking up in the recovery room and getting violently ill from the drugs they had used to put me to sleep. I was hoping for a better result this time. I hated the nausea that always accompanied me post-surgery.

New to me was the way they had me rest in a moveable recliner, not a regular hospital gurney or bed. I was placed in a slightly reclining position, where the nurses were already busy at work in getting my I.V. and shot ports prepared.

Just as planned, the anesthesiologist came to explain what meds and procedures they would use soon to get me ready for my surgery. It wasn't long until a nurse came in to give me the "happy" shot to put me to sleep.

My family was there all around me in the prep room, so that made me feel confident of their prayers and support. It was time to take the biggest step of my life. No more waiting. My surgery was about to get underway at last.

I barely remember them rolling me and my recliner into the operating room. Nothing but blackness settled in around me. I didn't feel a thing or notice anything at all until a couple of hours later in the recovery room.

It took me another half hour or so to really get my bearings back. The unusual thing was that I encountered not one bit of nauseous after this surgery. That was an awesome plus to me. My mind was telling me that maybe God was sending me a sign that this surgery was not going to be like the rest I had endured in my past. At the very least, it was starting off that way.

After a while they moved me into my private room, the place I would be stationed for the next three days. I remember a steady stream of friends and church members coming to visit and to extend their good wishes to me. The surgery didn't seem to be that rough, but moving around and trying to walk again was another thing.

I didn't really care for the every four-hour shot directly in my stomach. This was a precautionary step to keep me from getting blood clots (especially in my legs) while I was still very immobile. The shots didn't hurt all that much, but just the thought of a needle going directly into my mid-section, made me cringe.

Another downside of being post-op was the difficulty I had, especially at my size, to pull myself up into the sitting position in bed. Then it was even harder to push myself up into a standing position, as well. The day before surgery I had weighted-in at the perfectly "round" number of 300 pounds.

It wasn't too bad walking when they tried to get me up and moving again, but it was a hassle having to pull my I.V. stand along with me. I have always been a fighter, so if the doctor told me that I could get out of the hospital sooner if I would get up and walk more frequently, than that was what I had my mind set to do. Pain or not, I was going to walk myself up and down those hospital halls in the effort to get back home as soon as possible.

In my current situation, the very hardest thing for me to do was getting down to sit on the toilet. It was extremely painful, and I had to ask for help, which was a very humiliating thing to go through. But, as always, when you're a patient in a hospital, you must check your dignity in at the doorstep, because you'll never know what you might have to do or have done to you while there.

Another thing that I recall very vividly is the way my mouth would dry-out. I would have visitors come in, and I could barely talk. My lips kind of kept sticking to my teeth. No matter how many times I asked for ice or water, my liquid intake was very limited and most of the time my standard answer from my nurse on duty was "no" to more liquids this soon.

By the third day after surgery, I was really starting to get hungry. They finally brought me some clear broth, which was certainly not good, but at least it was something. The funny thing was that even though I felt famished, I could only take a few sips of broth until I was full. I was feeling very good about my non-desire to keep on eating.

On day four I was elated to be released from the hospital and to be traveling the short distance back home. I thought that being home would make me sleep better, but that was not the case at all. In fact, I had a lot more trouble trying to get up and down in our lower king-size bed. Also, I had to walk further to our large master bathroom.

The most annoying thing was that I had to have a pillow applied to my mid-section for support. It helped the pain when I was in a reclining position. Sleep was so hard to obtain the first few nights home, that I was back to trying to sleep in my old recliner. This brought back the painful reminder of sleepless nights attributed to acid reflux and the bleeding ulcers.

It was also a task to be able to swallow all the many vitamin supplements that I was required to take. Some were awful tasting powder vitamins, and others when swallowed, left a terrible after-taste in your mouth.

Pre-surgery, my doctor had taken me off a medicine to help me with my arthritis and tendonitis problems. He explained that this type of harsh medication would be too hard on my new, small stomach, and it also could harm my liver in the long run. He decided that I must give up these anti-inflammatory meds, and that after some time had passed, I wouldn't need them anyway with the luxury of my future weight-loss.

I had called these meds my "miracle" pills. When I took one of the tablets every day, I basically had no more joint pain in my knees, ankles, and feet. In years past, I had endured numerous heel spurs that were so painful that I had to take cortisone shots directly in the bottom of my feet to relieve at least some of the pain. When I didn't take that pill, then I could count on having trouble walking that day because of the excruciating pain.

At home, one night after surgery, I lowered myself into my garden bathtub and thought everything was fine. About thirty minutes later when I tried to get out of the tub, I experienced such pain that I couldn't manage to get myself up and out. I had to scream and scream, for what seemed like an eternity, before I could get the attention of my husband in another room watching TV. He finally arrived to help me get upright and out of the tub.

I immediately got dressed for bed and then hysterically called my surgeon. I asked him what had happened to make me unable to move myself without terrible pain. He reminded me about the heavy arthritis medicine he had taken me off, because it would be too harsh for my new stomach. He reminded me that now I would have to exercise every day to keep my body moving without that type of drug. If I didn't get myself ambulatory soon, then I would have to get used to the constant arthritic pain in my joints. The next morning, I started trying to walk a little every day. And the doctor proved to be right. The prescribed walking kept me from being so sore and worn-out.

Seven days after surgery, it was time for me to visit my doctor for a one-week checkup. I was so anxious to see how much weight I had already lost since my big operation day. The nurse led me back to check my blood pressure and weight. I took a deep breath and stepped on my lifetime nemesis, the scales. I almost passed-out when I realized that I had only lost two pounds. You talk about a major let down...... You mean that I'd gone through all this drastic surgery for a measly two-pound weight-loss?

The nurse then directed me to the doctor's examination room. He opened the door and I immediately asked him why I had only lost two pounds. He tried to calm me down and then assured me that it was because of all the fluids they had pumped into my body while I was in the hospital for four days. He went on to tell me that I just needed to give it some time.

After a couple of weeks after surgery, I was already sick of taking-in only liquids. Chicken broth, beef broth, chicken broth, beef broth.... By now it all tasted the same to me. The delight of my day was eating a sugar-free Popsicle. I would never have believed that one Popsicle could happily replace the nothingness of the broths.

Also, it was almost impossible for me to wash-down the required eight glasses of water every day. I felt like I was a floating blimp. And that meant that I had to walk even more to go back and forth to the bathroom. At this point, I wasn't too sure that I had made a good decision to go through with this surgery. But then again, I had to undergo the surgery to correct the bleeding ulcer anyway, so I guess it really didn't matter too much if the doctor had tried to help me out by adding-in the gastro bypass procedure at the same time. I had no choice but to listen to the advice of my doctor and give it some more time. Nevertheless, I was severely disappointed.

The weeks began to quick pass more quickly, and every day seemed to be getting easier for me. It wasn't long until I could tell that my body was dropping massive amounts of fat, and at a very rapid rate. After a couple of months had passed, I was able to cross my legs for the first time in years. It felt so comfortable and normal to sit with my legs crossed. If you've never been extremely overweight, then you don't realize what a luxury it is to be able to do something as common as crossing your legs. It is such a wonderful way to be able to sit.

A few more months later I noticed something drastically different when bathing. First, I felt so tiny in that previously compacted area called a bathtub. It was so amazing to see water rushing all around my body. Previously my huge legs and rump had blocked the water from traveling from the front to the back of the tub. But it had been years since I had been able to see the bones in my knees either. Before, there had been so much fat around them that I couldn't see any bone definition at all.

But much to my dismay, one day I discovered something eye-catchingly wrong with my left knee while I was sitting in the bathtub. Problem one: My left knee would not push down flat on the bottom surface of the tub. My right knee did this naturally, but not the left one. Problem two: I now noticed a huge raised knot on the inside top of my left knee. Its appearance was notably different than the right knee.

I was so ecstatic at my quick weight-loss that I wasn't going to worry about my weird left knee right now. (Another surgery would be required on down the line. I would need knee replacement. I thought this was ironic, as my knee didn't give me trouble when I was 300+ pounds, but now that I was exercising regularly, I had damaged it.) I was just so excited to be able to visually see the bones in that part of my body sticking out, just as if I was becoming a normal person.

By four months out of surgery, my clothes were beginning to hang on me. As an obese person for so many years, I was used to fitting into either tight-fitting clothes that bound me, or my other alternative was wearing what I termed "fat lady" clothing. My description of this type of day wear was over-sized and sloppy, and usually with big, ugly patterns that just screamed out, "Look at me in my unstylish fat lady clothes!"

For years I had despised going into "fat lady" stores like "Catherine's" and the "Avenue", but they were about the only stores that went up to the huge size that I had grown into, size 30-32 (or a "4X"). Yes, their styles and selections had improved over the years, but I still thought of their apparel as fat, cookie-cutter designs. I had a vast amount of their type of clothing hanging in my closet. I'm not putting these stores down, but to me their clothes often looked very similar, but just in different colors.

It was a true blessing that Amber had kept most of her old clothing as she took her weight-loss journey in 2010. As I lost more weight, she would send me home with loads of smaller-sized clothing. This literally saved me hundreds of dollars. I was losing so much weight in such an incredible amount of time that I would barely get to enjoy the newest batch of pants and blouses that she had given me. It began to seem that within another three to six-week time period, I was ready for the next smaller items she had saved back for me.

Amber herself, over a year and a half's time, had gone from 340 pounds to around 140. Her size in clothing unbelievably went from 26, down to size 4 or 6. I still couldn't get over her different appearance almost every time I saw her. She didn't even closely resemble the former fat daughter that I had known and loved so much of her life.

I, on the other hand, had decided not to weigh too often, because it always seems to disappoint me. In fact, I really didn't own scales. Previously I had not wanted to willingly see the degree of my depression in numbers. Therefore, after surgery, I would just check my weight at Amber's house occasionally. She now proudly owned scales.

I was absolutely delighted when I realized that I had already lost around 100 pounds about the time Christmas rolled around. That meant that it had only been almost six months since my surgery had taken place in July. Already I was looking so much better and feeling like I had so much more energy with every passing day.

By spring I had become quite the "Garage Sale Queen", because now I could find good, cheap clothing in human sizes. It was wonderful finding things that were nice, they fit, and were such good bargains.

One day I happened upon some children-size clothing at a local garage sale. I was so busy going through the items for some of my older granddaughters that I literally tripped over some old-time scales. I haphazardly asked the lady in charge of the sale if she could tell me how much she wanted for the scales. I admitted to her that I had not owned scales in years, and she asked why. I boldly told her that I had weighed over 300 pounds, but that I had undergone weight-loss surgery and lost a bunch of weight.

She said in response, "Good for you, girl. Take the scales free of charge. You deserve to have a free set of scales to weigh yourself on now."

So, I took my own scales home and then started monitoring my weight about once a week. A couple of months after my one-year anniversary of my surgery had passed, I recorded my lowest weight since high school days. Before we left for our Disney Cruise with Amber and her family, I weighed-in at the unfathomable amount of 145 pounds. This was certainly more weight-loss than I had ever dreamed of. I had always felt that I would be A-OK with being less than 200 pounds, but to realize that I now weighed half of what I weighed before surgery (300), was too incredible to truly believe.

CHAPTER 23

My Heroes Have Always Been Cowboys

Perhaps you'll remember the old Willie Nelson song called, "My Heroes Have Always Been Cowboys" from 1980. That has sort of been my life motto, in a strange kind of way.

In looking back now, my family has always loved football. My father enjoyed spending Friday nights supporting our local high school team, so I was introduced to it when I was in the first grade. We regularly attended home games, but often I would talk my father into a family road trip to support our Tigers when they played games away from our hometown.

Even as a small child, I would talk football with the best of the men members of my family. Usually I could memorize the players' names, positions, and their jersey numbers. I even had a best friend named Denise that also loved our high school football. It didn't matter that we were still in elementary school; we were just crazy about our football team. She and I would spend hour upon hour cutting up confetti, painting signs, and decorating our cowbells and other important noisemakers and sports paraphernalia. We would do anything to show support for our team. Even in the early sixties, I was obsessed with football.

I think it was so odd that much later in my life, in the late eighties, I happened upon one of my favorite high school heroes somewhat by "divine" intervention. I had started to attend a new Baptist church and sought to become more involved by joining their large choir.

After several weeks of coming to Wednesday night choir practice, I happened to overhear someone trying to catch one of the men in the choir as he left the music building. I heard the name of "Tommy Horton" called out and immediately snapped to attention. I saw the man come back into the room. He and another gentleman finished their conversation, and I waited just outside the door to catch him as he started for his car.

"Mr. Horton?" I asked.

He quickly responded, "Yes. How can I help you?"

I was kind of embarrassed to front the guy, but I had gotten this far so I felt I had to keep on going with my line of questioning.

"I hate to bother you, but are you Tommy Horton, #10, that used to be the quarterback for the Lancaster Tiger football team?"

He kind of grinned and turned a bit red, but then shyly answered, "Yes. That would be me."

I told him how he had been my favorite player back in the mid-sixties. I explained how my family had followed the Tigers when he was at the helm of the team back then. I finished our conversation by saying that it had been a pleasure meeting him. I was so thrilled that I had the opportunity to meet one of my all-time favorite high school football heroes.

A few months later we mysteriously found ourselves living next door to each other. In fact, our families became good friends and we lived as next-door neighbors for a several years. And it was even more strange still that his daughter and mine (Buffy) became best friends and teammates on the same high school basketball team.

I also thought irony played a part again as I found myself employed as the personal secretary of a former NFL football player. In the eighties, my boss was Bill Glass. He was a great defensive end in the late fifties and over much of the sixties. He played for both the Detroit Lions and the Cleveland Browns. After a successful collegiate and pro career, he retired and started his own Christian ministry. He excelled in leading a prolific prison organization and a very successful city-wide ministry, as well. He also traveled much of his time as a professional motivational speaker and authored several books.

I was so in awe of this giant-of-a-man. He had the largest hands I had ever seen in my life. I was often scared of him and his size. I sometimes thought…. "Wow! If I do something wrong and he gets mad at me, he might just take one of those big "paws" and take a swipe at me."

Bill turned-out to be a rather "gentle giant", and I soon realized that I had nothing to fear because of his weight and stature. In fact, all of us ladies in the office thought it was quite humorous that his petite 90-pound wife would often come bounding into our building and start ordering him around like she was a drill sergeant. He was so smitten with her, that he would do whatever she told him to do --- no questions asked. Everyone could easily tell who lovingly wore the pants in the family.

I did love the fact that many of Bill's fundraising banquets included yearly affairs that featured the likes of sports figures like Ivan "Pudge" Rodriquez and Jim Sundberg of the Texas Rangers baseball team, as well as Kyle Rote, Jr., a famous pro soccer player for the Dallas Tornado. It was so exciting getting to meet football people like Mike Barber, tight end for the Houston Oilers, and other greats like quarterback Roger Staubach and Coach Tom Landry of the Dallas Cowboys – just to name a few. I really enjoyed the chance to interact with some of these sports stars, but what I really treasured most was getting the honor of typing Bill's book manuscripts over the span of time from 1983 through 1988.

I was so envious of Bill's ability to write and to successfully have books published all the time. This was the profession I had wanted to be a part of for most of my life. It was such a great learning experience for me, but after a great run it was time to make a career change. I had become tired of being a secretary. I wanted to find something where I could use my writing skills more effectively.

In keeping with the fanatic "football-ism" in my life, I must admit that my entire family simply adored the Dallas Cowboys pro football team, and that was putting it lightly. As I admitted previously, I became a die-hard Dallas Cowboy fan back in the inaugural days of the team in the sixties. I was addicted at the tender age of seven years old. Some of my first Cowboy heroes were players like Don Meredith, Bob Lilly, Chuck Howley, Don Perkins, and Bob Hayes.

I couldn't believe how "cool" my mother was when she was younger. I'll never forget her taking us to some Dallas area department store locations where some of my favorite football heroes were signing autographs. These advertised areas were overrun with crazed Cowboys fans. The lines for those coveted autographs were long and tiring.

My mother got the biggest kick out of watching my sister get mad and red-faced because some of the people in her line to see quarterback Don Meredith were pushing and shoving. Finally, Mr. Meredith saw what was happened, so he called my sister Brenda up to the front of the line and jokingly remarked, "I'm going to sign your autography right now, 'cause I can't stand to see the pained look on your face".

We were Cowboys fans through the heart, so whatever we had to do to get an autograph, we deemed it "worth it".

My parents were particularly huge Cowboy fans, which meant that my sister and I became fans, which meant that I would marry a man that was a Cowboy fan, which meant that our daughters would inevitably be Cowboys fans. And, so, our passion for Cowboy football has been passed down from generation to generation, and even until this day.

One of my greatest heartthrobs of all time was #41, cornerback/safety Charlie Waters. He played for the Cowboys from 1970 to 1981. I thought he was such a cute, little moppy-headed guy that so infamously sat on the sidelines upon his helmet, when he was not in the game as a defensive back.

I recall being so infatuated with him that I had photos and newspaper articles on the front and back of my school notebook. He would brighten-up my day, just by my looking down and seeing him. I carried him around to all my classes every school day. I know.....I was such a football nerd.

One of the best surprises of my life came early one, crisp fall morning in Irving, Texas. Don and I were now married, and we both had the day off work for some reason. Perhaps it was a national holiday of some sort—Labor Day, I think. All I know is that we had decided to get up super-early that Monday morning to meet some sports talk personalities in the vicinity of the old Texas Stadium, where the Dallas Cowboys played and called home at the time.

We were excited to be at the "live" sportscast that began at 5:30 a.m. We were there mainly because they were giving away free tickets for that very night, as the Cowboys were going to be featured on "Monday Night Football" in Chicago, Illinois. As luck would have it, we didn't win the trip to Chicago and the tickets to the game that evening, but I received a much better surprise.

The football "love of my life" was on location that morning —and in the flesh, there was my beloved Charlie Waters. He was just as handsome as ever, and even more polished since he was now an older, mid-forties gentleman, that had already retired from the Cowboy team. He spoke to the crowd for about twenty minutes that morning and I hung on his every word.

If you know what a great sports fan I am, then you understand that I couldn't leave this situation alone. I HAD to go and meet this hero of mine. Don was so totally embarrassed, but I was not going to let this chance slip through my hands. Straight up to Mr. Waters I went. I then asked him for his autograph, and proudly told him how, back in the day, he had been properly displayed on my high school notebook – all four years at Lancaster High School. I could tell how impressed he was about this fact (NOT!), but I had to share my memory with him anyway.

Don said that I couldn't wipe the smile off my face for about a week! What an honor for me to get to meet him in person!

In fact, this brings me to another football remembrance concerning my daughters Amber and Buffy and myself. I distinctly remember back to a time after the year 2000 when we jokingly referred to ourselves as "the answer" to owner Jerry Jones' offensive line problems. He never seemed to have enough "beefy" personnel up front to sufficiently block for our running backs. Maybe Jones should have taken a serious look at us Hullett girls. All three of us were well over 300 pounds, and he could have had us blocking for a lot less money than some of these smaller-type pansy linemen he had signed over the years. LOL

One of the biggest deals of my "football" kind of life was that I realized that most of my adult years I had spent on this earth enduring the infamous notoriety of weighing more than every man on the entire roster of the Dallas Cowboys. Where some of these guys were "huge" by football standards, their average weight would have probably been between 200 and 300 pounds. These extremely heavy men usually were six-foot-tall, or even bigger in height.

However, at my highest weight, I was 340 pounds and was only 5 feet 4 inches tall. Oh, how I had wanted to -- at least -- weigh less than these monster-size football players. Thankfully, that lofty goal was obtained in October of 2012. No more comparisons to NFL football players, ever again! I still love my Dallas Cowboys with all my heart, but I just don't want to be as big as one of them.

CHAPTER 24

"It's Not Over Until the Fat Lady Sings"

And I haven't sung yet.......

My son-in-law Boyd says that Amber and I took the easy way out on weight-loss. He feels that we somehow "cheated" by going through a weight-loss surgery, but I beg to differ. Is there ever really an easy way to lose weight – especially when a person has 50 pounds, 100 pounds, or even a much larger amount of weight to lose down to be considered a normal size? And the hardest part of the losing is keeping it off. I can attest to that from the 500+ pounds that I've lost over the course of my lifetime.

All I can tell anyone from my experiences is that you've got to keep up the fight -- because it's worth it. I wouldn't trade all the pain and trials for what I got back in return. I feel like another person has been lifted off my shoulders, and that is exactly what happened to me. To think that I shed 150 pounds is unfathomable to me.

No wonder I feel healthier and happier today. No more sleep apnea, no more back pain, no more aching knees, no more cortisone foot injections for heel spurs, no more orthotic shoe inserts, no more diabetic medications (after I had lost a chunk of my weight, my primary care physician declared that I no longer need diabetic meds), no more huffing and puffing while walking up and down stairs, no more chapped fat legs, no more heavy breathing when I rush to answer the phone, no more trouble finding clothes that fit, no more paranoia over people looking at me, no more worries of whether I can fit in a seat, or no more worries that I might break the chair that I choose to sit on, etc. But more importantly, *"Fatty Patty"* doesn't live inside my head any more. I am not the perfect body, nor the perfect picture of health, but I am proud to say that I am a much better version of the "morbidly obese" Patty.

The most endearing thing that came out of MY surgery was probably not something "special" that most overweight people would appreciate. No, I was not enthralled with my new body because I thought I was a better-looking person. And, no, I wasn't thinking I was sexy in my new skin. And, no, I wasn't hoping to gain other people's attention due to my drastic transformation.

I am simply thrilled to death that my grandkids now come running up to me, and they can put their arms around all of me. It is one of the greatest joys of my life. The granddaughters especially comment often how "skinny" I am now and how they love to "hug me all the way". I thank you, Lord Jesus, for this blessing in my life.

I recently found the following adage posted in Facebook from an unknown author, and it goes like this......

"The most precious jewels you'll ever have around your neck are the arms of your grandchildren."

That is truly how I feel now that an extra person has been lifted from my body.

Yes, there were a lot of things that I went through and that I am still experiencing because of going through such a dangerous and dramatic weight-loss surgery, but I would do it again in a heartbeat. In fact, I only wish that I had had the courage to try the surgery years earlier, and maybe I would have had even more enjoyable, active years with my husband, daughters, and grandchildren.

However, I am now confident that, Lord willing, He has granted me some extra years of living on this earth, as the path I was headed down with my obesity, was not looking promising. My family doctor often reminded me that at my previous weight of 300 plus pounds, I was like a ticking, time bomb. What would be my cause of death???? Could it be a heart attack (as my father's first heart attack occurred at age 41) or a stroke (like my mother suffered at age 55)?

Or, according to the Highland Hospital Bariatric Surgery Center website -- (*"MORBID OBESITY IS A SERIOUS HEALTH CONDITION"*). Their experts say that *"Those who are morbidly obese are at greater risk for illnesses including diabetes, high blood pressure, sleep apnea, gastro esophageal reflux disease (GERD), gallstones, osteoarthritis, heart disease, and cancer."* This list is not a team that I want to be a part of, do you?

A few years ago, my previous church pastor asked his parishioners to go to a website called "deathclock.com". You can plug-in your birthdate, your lifestyle type, and your BMI (Body Mass Index) --- and the website will estimate the date of your impending death. I kind of chuckled, back before my weight-loss surgery, because according to my morbidly obese BMI, I was already DEAD. Now that my BMI has changed drastically, I am happy to report that this "guessing" life-expectancy website now shows that I should still have 30 to 35 more years on this earth. That is truly a positive take on my decision to undergo and successfully complete my second weight-loss surgery.

I'll never forget some of the harsh things that happened to me because of being overweight. Here is a prime example of why I often felt so damaged.

When I was in-between jobs in my thirties, a distant cousin told my aunt that she worked at a law firm and she could probably get me a position at her law firm, but she said, "I don't think Patty could make it up our long flight of stairs to the second floor."

Of course, my aunt told my mother, and my mother told me. I was crushed at how handicapped she thought I must be!

Back to "present-day, real time"...... About a year ago, the same cousin wrote on Face Book. "I hate it when I see a fat mother and her fat little kids trailing behind her in the grocery store, putting nothing but a bunch of junk food in their shopping cart. People like that make me sick!" WHAT kind of person says things like that?????

Well, I couldn't hold my tongue any longer. I answered her on Face Book, telling her that fat people have feelings, too, and that no one ENJOYS being fat.

I even brought up her statement from years ago, about me being too fat to get up the stairs at her law office. I informed her that back in the 80s, I was busy teaching baton twirling lessons 3 times a week, I coached one of my daughter's soccer teams, and I played coed softball for my church. So, so much for her theory that I was a complete "couch potato". Nothing could have been further from the truth. Being fat didn't mean that I was lazy.

That still infuriates me when people who have never had a weight problem, try to make fun or give suggestions on how to be "skinny". They absolutely have no idea what it feels like and how hard it truly is losing weight.

Despite some of the negative things that happened, as I grew older and matured, I gained even more confidence in myself. Thankfully, my mother had taught me well that I, alone, held the key to choosing to let my obesity become a handicap in my life, or not. She pounded in my head that I could do, or be, or accomplish anything I set my mind to, and I believed her.

As a result, I was always a kind of over-achiever. I was relentless about being the best at whatever I tried to do. Do you know what kind of pressure that puts on yourself? I was constantly trying to be "perfect", and there is no such thing as someone being "perfect" in this life. Jesus was the only perfect one that walked the earth where we live.

So, my past behind me, I took the plunge and went through my second weight-loss surgery in 2011, but here are……..

A FEW THINGS THE DOCTORS FORGOT TO TELL ME ABOUT....

However, here are some things I was not prepared for with my extreme life-changing operation. Once I had lost the biggest portion of my weight and really "looked" into my mirror, it became abundantly aware that I "looked" much older in the face. I can totally understand that part of my transformation. When you are very fat and your face is stretched to its fullest potential, there are no real wrinkles to be found. Once most of the fat was gone from my face, I, for the first time in my life, had to acknowledge that I did look somewhat older. That's ok by me. I willingly was alright with a few years added to my facial features. I also understood the reason why.

Looking back, no one told me that I would have inches and inches of loose skin hanging from my upper arms (some of my grandkids tell me that I have "bat wings"!), from my stomach area, and from my deflated thighs. Previously my husband had lovingly named the huge legs that Amber and me had (in our former lives) as "thankles". You've probably guessed by now that he was defining our super-sized thighs that practically went from the top of our legs down to the ankle area. Thankfully, Amber and I no longer have "thankles".

All I know is that the poor skin covering my body had been stretched and reduced so many times that it must have felt like a musical accordion. It had no idea of what I ever had in store for it. During the overweight years, I was constantly roller-coaster dieting.

In addition to other weight-loss changes, I had no idea that I would have to learn new ways to sleep and to sit with a much different sized body. I was totally amazed to find that bony knees aren't conducive to my sleeping while laying on my left or right side. It was often just plain painful. Bone on bone was a new concept to me. And, to reiterate again, the ability to now cross my much-thinner legs was a complete joy in my life.

What I most hated was the fact that during my first year of weight-loss my good, thick hair started falling-out. I'd have to change my pillow case almost daily because of all the hair I was shedding. I even had to part my hair on the other side of my head because I had a very noticeable bald spot. (My doctor explained to me that my hormones were raging and my body was in complete shock from so many quick changes in my internal systems.)

It also hadn't occurred to me that I would go from a hot-natured, sweating person, to one that is often cold and in the need of a sweater or jacket (almost year-around, and in the great HOT State of Texas). I was never hardly ever cold before. After my surgery I generally don't sweat much at all anymore. Also, my feet are smaller so I can wear a smaller size shoe. And no more sticky, sweating feet, a wonderful trait that I had inherited from my daddy. Foot odor --- now gone!

Speaking of gone, my boobs were almost non-existent after surgery. As a general rule, a really heavy female usually has a pretty buxom chest, and that is mainly because she gets the added "advantage" of her back-fat filtering-in from underneath her arms and ending up in her bra cups. In my case, I went from a 50-DD to a 40B. And now I know why there are so many choices when deciding on a padded bra. I told myself that I'd never have need of a "Victoria's Secret" shop, but I have learned to never say "never". Technically, female breasts are largely made up of "fat" tissue and "fat" cells, so I guess I don't understand men's obsession with boobs. They are really just lumps of "fat". However, their size reduces as a result of losing weight. When a woman is burning fat, she is burning fat in her breasts as well. Such is the case in reverse. When you gain weight, your breasts grow larger. Before my surgery I had trouble finding a big enough bra to fit me, both in cup size and in the width size of the bra to go around my large frame. The need for an ungodly-sized bra is no longer a problem I have to worry about.

Also, I experienced a problem every time I shaved under my arms. Amber is right there with me on this dilemma. Both of us, because of the extreme amount of weight that we've lost, have bone structure (under our arms) so hollow there now, that we have trouble shaving without cutting ourselves. Our underarms are now extremely concave.

Another problem I face even today is that I sometimes detest that my mouth starts watering and I suddenly feel the urge to vomit. Either I have not chewed-up the food well enough, or it might be a food that is hard for my stomach to tolerate, or I might be putting too much food in my body at one time. This is usually a tale-tale sign that I need to stop eating immediately. I do not gag myself any longer like after my previous surgery. I usually just walk a bit and the bad feeling passes in a few minutes.

What is ultra-strange is that Amber underwent a completely different style of weight-loss surgery from me. I laugh when she starts repeatedly sneezing toward the end of a meal. This function is her "cut-off" valve that her stomach is full. Isn't that an odd way that her body tells her to stop cramming food into her body? Her sneezing is her official stop sign.

Amber and I both go through the same challenges as we now shop for regular-sized clothing. In our previous fat days, it was much, much easier to shop. We went directly to the back corner of the "women's world" or "plus-size" wear, and there was usually only a rack or two of clothes to choose from in our ungodly sizes. And our previous choice for a clothes item was divided into two simple categories: it fits, or it doesn't fit.

Today we are totally overwhelmed at huge department stores. There are so many shopping considerations to deal with --- by style, by designer name, by seasons, by color schemes, etc. It's almost like we have trouble deciding on one selection because we really don't know what our "style" is now. Amber hates to go shopping alone these days, as she says that she still thinks of herself as a "fat" person and she says that she can't tell if something looks good on herself or not. I guess I don't understand that, as in my mind her current size is tiny by my standards. And I always think that she looks fabulous because of her astonishing weight-loss, no matter what she is wearing.

Don and I are so very proud of our daughter Amber. And my mother felt (I lost my mom in May 2014) the same way about my weight-loss. It's just a parent / child kind of thing that is so satisfying for your offspring to finally achieve success, especially when it concerns his/her general health and longevity.

CHAPTER 25

The Purpose of My Life

As I journey through my daily life with a regular-sized body, I now see more and more overweight people all around me --- be it children or adults. They are everywhere you look. It is a growing and alarming thing that is becoming more and more common in America. I can only think that much of the obesity problem stems from our more cram-packed lifestyles today where "fast food" is king. Many folks often choose convenience over healthy food choices, me included. It's so much easier to just drive-thru, grab something, and then choke it down in a hurry. In addition, we (or our children) often choose to be involved in activities in the evening, and then we put off eating until 8:00 or 9:00 p.m. There's nothing like eating a heavy dinner or some high-calorie fast food, and then going on to bed shortly thereafter. That can really pack the pounds on quickly.

Also, when I was kid, we played outside from almost sunup until sundown. These days, kids can't play outside much, without the chaperoning adult (or parents, or babysitters, or siblings) there in place to watch over them. Kids don't have the same freedoms that I had when I was growing up, and especially in the summer time. My sister and I would go off riding bicycles all over our town. We often traveled several miles from the northern-most part of our city, to the southern-most area to go to our local swimming pool. We would spend four to six hours swimming almost daily, and then ride the couple of miles back home alone in the late afternoon. We also

157

frequently rode our bikes or walked to the public library that was always quite a way off from our home. It's true that kids can't really be kids these days, not the way we had enjoyed our time-off from school in the summer. Too much mischief and meanness is going on around us all the time.

Now-a-days the kids often stay inside all day and watch TV, play computer games, involve themselves in home entertainment applications, etc. They often become overweight children and dreaded couch potatoes instead of healthy, active kids. It is a sad commentary of the world in which we live today. Sometimes inactive children become overweight children with all types of physical and mental problems that they didn't willingly sign-up for. Sadly, it's a sign of the times in the 21st century.

Here is a poem that I wrote about the sad truth of the children of today.

POEM --- "Kids Today"
By Patty Hullett, 03/02/17

What is up with our kids today?
They never seem to go out and play.
From the time they wake and see the sun,
Their lives are scheduled, no time for fun.

It's lessons or sports or watching TV,
They hope to be entertained by what they see,
There's no such thing as riding their bike,
Or taking a lunch and going on a hike.

Today even the youngsters are glued to their phones,
Watching things that parents shouldn't condone,
Apps and games are now taking the place,
As substitutes for basic manners and grace.

When I was a kid I loved to be outdoor,
Being locked inside the house was such a bore,
We played with neighbors till time to come in,
Then the next day we'd enjoy the same things again.

We walked, rode bikes and loved jumping rope,
Our days were filled with friendship and hope.
Sometimes we played in the nasty old creek,
And our favorite game was "hide and go seek".

We picked up coke bottles and walked to the store,
Cashed them in to buy candy galore.
It was so much fun just playing pretend,
When the street lights came on, our playtime had to end.

But today…...things are so different…...

It's much too scary to let the children outside,
And they can't walk to school, they must have a ride.
No more biking through neighborhoods to find a ball game,
And in the big schools, no one cares to know your name.

Before -- no worries about bombs or things like firearms,
The biggest problem we had was someone pulling the fire alarms.
Yes, things weren't perfect, but I certainly was never scared
About a senseless school shooting or suicide that left a classmate dead.

These days parents sacrifice guidance all the while,
For keeping up with the Jones, is what's more in style,
Will our robotic children become obsolete?
Or will we wake-up and get off our seats?

Let us move off the couches and take them outside,
To get involved in their lives and guide them with pride,
I know this is not easy, and it will surely take some time,
But your kids are certainly worth it, and peace you may find,
To help them regain, their safe childhood is the key,
Results -- kids that are healthy and happy as can be.

I have always been a people-watcher, but often I now watch "fat" people. When I see a very overweight person in front of me, I immediately empathize for them. I can almost tell from the countenance on his/her face that they are hurting as they walk by. It could be feet problem causing them pain, or knees hurting, or back aching, etc. I can't really pin-point the source of their pain, but I can just tell that they are physically hurting. When I come across people that are tremendously overweight, I genuinely "hurt" for them, because I know exactly how it feels to be morbidly obese and often miserable in their own bodies.

One thing my daddy told me growing up was that "you don't have to remind a fat person that they are fat, they already know it and don't need to constantly be reminded of it". And no matter how much of a class clown, a life of the party, or a roll-off-the shoulders kind of person you think you might be, I am confident that deep down in your heart, you don't really want to be overweight. You either don't know how to correct the problem, or perhaps you've tried before and didn't succeed.

Some people may be like I was. I had tried so many different types of weight-loss methods and failed, that I had basically given up and just stopped trying at all. I didn't want to face my critics again, knowing that behind my back they were most liking thinking, "She's blown off the diet again and gained all of her weight back." This idea of negatively failing at my weight-loss, yet again, always made me feel more defeated than before I had started the diet. I certainly didn't want anyone to pity me.

During my countless years spent as a fat person, I can't tell you how many times people would come up to me and say something along the lines of .... "You are so pretty in your face". I assume that they were meaning this comment as a valid compliment, but I guess I took it the wrong way. In my mind what they were saying meant, "I think you are OK as a fatty, but at least you have one last redeeming quality, in that you at least are not horribly ugly." Either way I might look at this statement, it still often left me with something more akin to shame. If the person was attempting to make me feel better about being obese, it had definitely NOT made me feel any better. Nice try, but no cigar!

Much to my daughter Amber's chagrin, she often tells me that I place much too much importance on a person's "size". After going back to my family doctor for a yearly examination twelve month after my weight-loss procedure, I discussed this very valid point with my physician. I tried to explain my "fat" feelings and how they are tied to my mental psyche. I also described how Amber didn't think the weight-loss thing should be a big deal for either of us in our future lives.

My doctor made me realize what I already knew in my heart. Since I had been an overweight person for at least fifty years of my life, the "fatness" had become embedded into everything about me. Being "Fatty Patty" was really who I was, and in some ways, that I still am today.

He went on to say that Amber wouldn't be able to understand the depth of my attachment to "fat", the same way that she looked at it. She was much younger and had not gone through decade after decade with a persona like mine. So, I still will probably always be "Fatty Patty" in my mind, but I am so excited to know that she no longer rules me.

And if you are overweight and unhappy about it, then don't let anything stop you from trying to do something to change it. With God as my witness, it's for sure that I've tried almost everything under the sun to lose weight. Every person is different, and there are many, many ways of attempting weight-loss. Just keep in mind that you must never give up or stop trying. Keep the faith! It might take you fifty plus years (like me) to overcome your food addiction and/or your family heredity, but you can succeed if you keep on trying. I am living proof of that fact.

My cousin Selena recently posted a *"Face Book"* question that I consider to be very thought-provoking. "What were you in your previous life?" I considered this interesting thought for several minutes and posted in return, "I <u>WAS</u> a fat girl".

IN LOOKING BACK

In 2011, I felt like I might have stomach cancer. I seemed to feel sick all the time, and I was dropping some weight and losing a lot of blood. My stomach problems finally led me to an internal medicine doctor appointment.

This sweet Christian doctor told me, "I think you either have stomach cancer or ulcers, but we're going to pray that it's the ulcers".

A few days later, I was in the local hospital to have 70 percent of my stomach removed due to a huge ulcer the size of a baseball. My new hero, my internal medicine doctor, begged the surgeon to do a gastric bypass surgery at the same time, to help me lose weight. The surgeon didn't want to do the 2-for-1 procedure, but my favorite new doctor was relentless, until he finally got the surgeon to agree on doing the weight-loss bypass surgery as well.

Fifteen months later after my double-surgery, I had lost a total of 155 pounds. As a result, I am no longer taking diabetic medicines, I have no more heel problems, I am more mobile than I've been in years, and I feel like this procedure literally added years onto my life.

I am very proud to say that my Lord and Savior Jesus Christ, took a terrible medical problem and turned it into something good for me.

In retrospect, I was a fat 10-pound baby, a fat toddler, a fat elementary kid, a fat teenager, and a fat adult. Through all those years of being obese, I would often wonder why God made me fat. Here's my answer in a scripture that says it all......

Psalm 139:13-16 The Message (MSG)

13-16 Oh yes, you shaped me first inside, then out;
   you formed me in my mother's womb.
I thank you, High God—you're breathtaking!
   Body and soul, I am marvelously made!
   I worship in adoration—what a creation!
You know me inside and out,
   you know every bone in my body;
You know exactly how I was made, bit by bit,
   how I was sculpted from nothing into something.
Like an open book, you watched me grow from conception
to birth;
   all the stages of my life were spread out before you,
The days of my life all prepared
   before I'd even lived one day.

Isn't that amazing to think about how God made each one of us unique and different?

I think I know now why I've lived 50+ years as an overweight person. He gave me this obstacle to make me stronger and much more sensitive. He's taught me how to handle the kind of pain that comes from being "different". In actuality, being "fat" is who I am, and I'm no longer worried about what anybody else thinks of my outward appearance. To me, it's all about what's on the inside. I only have to please my Lord, and no one else.

I now realize that God has a purpose for my life. I knew from the time I was about junior high age, that I had a gift of writing, but for some reason, none of my man-made plans ever included me getting to do what I loved best – and that was writing.

Just in the past year (2017-2018), at the ripe old age of 63, I am retired but I am now a freelance writer, doing feature stories and sports coverage news for two local community newspapers. I have several children's books ready for possible publication. I almost have enough inspirational poems to complete a book of poetry.

In addition, I am now a certified public speaker for a national, Christian non-profit group called *"Stonecroft Ministries"*.

So, I'm beginning to figure-out my true purpose in life. I feel the Lord is leading me in the area of speaking to and encouraging ladies' groups or teenage girls. I hope to teach them about their own self-esteem and confidence – no matter what body size they have. My future goal is to become a traveling author and speaker, in my quest to impart the love and grace that only Jesus Christ can give to girls and women of all ages. Most need to hear (or hear again as an important reminder) that God looks at the heart first, not at our physical, outward appearance. So many times, we listen to the world in which we live. As a Christian lady, we shouldn't view our acceptance by comparison or by the way much of the secular world sees us as females.

So, today I am very proud of the new and improved Patty. I'm now a regular-sized person, and I don't hear those negative voices telling me that I'm not good enough anymore. I'm happy to just be me. And it's good to know that I have finally obtained a new level of confidence in the Lord, enough confidence to finally say, "Bye-bye, Fatty Patty!"

And one final motivating thought from Fatty Patty...... My God took something very bad (a bleeding stomach ulcer the size of a baseball) and turned it into something wonderful for me (a second weight-loss surgery that I didn't ask for, and one that was finally successful). To Him, I will always be eternally grateful. In fact, I think He gave me the greatest gift I've ever received (except for my salvation).

My "new life" scripture is now:

Romans 8:28 - New King James Version (NKJV)

[28] **And we know that all things work together for good to those who love God, to those who are the called according to *His* purpose.**

CPSIA information can be obtained
at www.ICGtesting.com
Printed in the USA
BVHW07*1018160718
521738BV00007B/92/P